CAMBRIDGE
ENGLISH
for schools
Workbook Two

ANDREW LITTLEJOHN & DIANA HICKS

CAMBRIDGE
UNIVERSITY PRESS

Published by the Press Syndicate of the University of Cambridge
The Pitt Building, Trumpington Street, Cambridge CB2 1RP
40 West 20th Street, New York, NY 10011-4211, USA
10 Stamford Road, Oakleigh, Melbourne 3166, Australia

© Cambridge University Press 1996

First Published 1996

Printed in Great Britain at the University Press, Cambridge.

ISBN 0 521 42174 8 Workbook
ISBN 0 521 42170 5 Student's Book
ISBN 0 521 42178 0 Teacher's Book
ISBN 0 521 42182 9 Class Cassette Set
ISBN 0 521 42131 4 Workbook Cassette

Contents

1 Welcome back!

1 Whose photographs are they?

Reading

Read what Vincent, Maria, Rick and Sujita say about their holidays.
Who do the photographs belong to?

Rick:

Vincent:

Maria:

Sujita:

> I had a great holiday at the seaside with my uncle. There are lots of different fish there. We were there two weeks.

> I went camping in the mountains with my family. It was wonderful! My brother jumped in the river with all his clothes on. It was so funny!

> I went camping, too, with my brother and some friends. We made a big house in the trees. It was great!

> I had a fantastic holiday. We went to London! There are many famous places there.

You can hear Vincent, Sujita, Maria and Rick on the cassette.

2 The world encyclopaedia

Reading and general knowledge

How much do you know about the world? Can you fill in the missing information?
(If you don't know, ask your family or friends.)

The world of people and places

This is Sydney. They speak .... there. Many people think Sydney is the capital of ...., but it·isn't. The capital is .... Sydney is a very beautiful city. Sydney is in the South-........................ of the country. It has a population of about .... million.

The Opera House, Sydney

The world of science

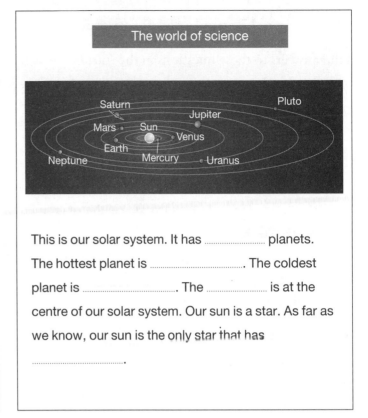

This is our solar system. It has .... planets. The hottest planet is .... The coldest planet is .... The .... is at the centre of our solar system. Our sun is a star. As far as we know, our sun is the only star that has

....

The world of history

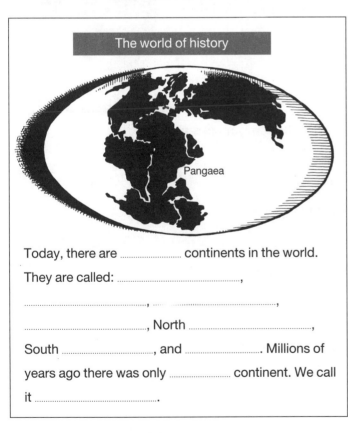

Pangaea

Today, there are .... continents in the world. They are called: ...., ..., ..., ..., North ...., South ...., and .... Millions of years ago there was only .... continent. We call it ....

The world of nature

There are five important types of animals. They are called mammals, reptiles, ..., ... and .... Mammals have .... blood and they give .... to their babies. Reptiles have .... blood and they lay eggs. .... have got six legs. Many of them can .... also lay eggs but they have feathers. The last type of animal is .... Their blood is .... and they live in water.

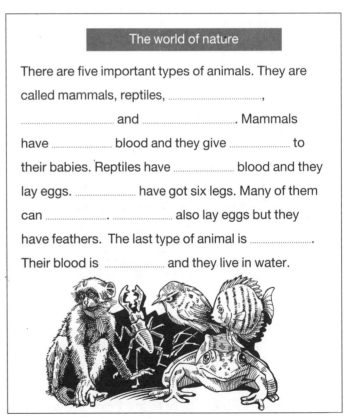

---

3 Write something for the encyclopaedia

Writing

What are you interested in – people and places, science, nature or history? Choose a topic and write part of the encyclopaedia. Include a photograph or a drawing. Write on a separate piece of paper.

4 The world encylopaedia puzzle

Vocabulary

Find answers to these questions in the square:

1 What is the capital of the United States of America?
2 When a metal gets hot, it ....
3 A whale is not a fish. It is a ....
4 Panda bears live in ..... .
5 Cave people hunted .... for food.
6 In which continent is Japan?
7 .... on the moon is much weaker than it is on Earth.
8 The Aztecs lived in ....

```
G H T G J I K I O P W E Q S F H G F G F
R H E Y G A H Y E H G A A S I A L F J A
A E T F A M K L B C Q W E S F A R O U N
V T F X M E X I C O M H N U T F E Q R I
I J W A S H I N G T O N T Q I D P R P M
T T H E R U D T R S T Y A J H S B I E A
Y K I O L P L K M N H B G V F C S S F L
E X P A N D S F T G Y H U J I K O E P S
H J U H Y A M A M M A L L E R T U I O U
F G T R F D E W S E D R F T C H I N A C
```

Write eight more questions. Make a word puzzle for other students to find the answers.

5 Talk to Peter

Writing and speaking

Write your answers to Peter's questions.

PETER: Hello! How are you?

YOU: ....

PETER: I was at the seaside last week. What did you do on your last holiday?

YOU: ....

PETER: That sounds interesting. Did you enjoy it?

YOU: ....

PETER: Next holiday, I want to go to the mountains. Are there mountains near you?

YOU: ....

PETER: There are some mountains near my home. They're in Scotland.
They have a lot of snow in the winter. Do you have snow?

YOU: ....

PETER: I must tell you something. My brother got a new car yesterday. It's
fantastic. What's new in your life?

YOU: ....

PETER: Oh, yes? That's interesting. Tell me more about it.

YOU: ....

PETER: Listen, I have to go. I can talk to you later. Bye!

Now talk to Peter on the cassette.

6 Sing a song! All around the world

See page 154 in your Student's Book
for the words to 'All around the world'.

2 Extension The world encyclopaedia

Optional revision exercises

Choose the parts that you need to do.
Look at the Test and Extension exercises on pages 13–22 in your Student's Book.

The world of people and places

1 In the snow and ice

Adjectives

Look at this picture. How can you describe it?
Put the adjectives under the right heading.

Words that describe the picture.

Words that don't describe the picture.

interesting wet cold dry snowy empty
exciting happy horrible hot nice rainy sunny
windy beautiful friendly tall ugly boring icy

Next lesson, compare your lists with other students'.

2 Antarctica

Reading

Antarctica is the coldest place on Earth, but people from all over the world come to work there. What do they do? Read and find out.

LIFE in the snow and ice

Near the South Pole, three thousand people live together in a place called Amundsen-Scott Station.

This is one of the driest and coldest places in the world. The station has libraries, cinemas, shops, sports rooms, canteens and laboratories. There is electricity, and they have telephones and computers.

But the people here don't travel by car, or train, or bus, because there aren't any roads or railways near the station. They travel by ship, helicopter, plane, or snow tractor, or with dogs.

There aren't any trees or flowers there, but there are hundreds of different birds and other animals.

Most of the people here are scientists. They study plant and animal life and how ice moves. The ice can tell us about changes in climate.

Amundsen-Scott Station doesn't have any factories. There aren't any children here so there aren't any schools or teachers. Ray Kingman is a scientist at the station.

'This is my second year here,' he says. 'It's a very interesting and beautiful place, but life is very hard in the winter. In the summer we can go swimming in hot pools of water. There are a lot of volcanoes near here, and the volcanoes heat the water for us. Sometimes the water is too hot!'

3 Possible or impossible?

Present simple negatives

Are these things possible or impossible? Write a sentence about each one.

a Ray goes to work on a train.
Impossible! Amundsen-Scott doesn't have any trains.

b Ray buys his food in the shop.
Possible! Amundsen-Scott has ....

c Ray's children go to school in Amundsen-Scott.
....

d Ray likes swimming in the swimming pool.
....

e Ray can telephone his family.
....

f After work every day Ray likes to work in his garden.
....

g The traffic is very bad in Amundsen-Scott.
....

h Sometimes there is too much rain in Amundsen-Scott.
....

The world of nature

4 What animal is it?

Present simple questions

Li and her friends are playing a game. Do you know what animal she is thinking of?

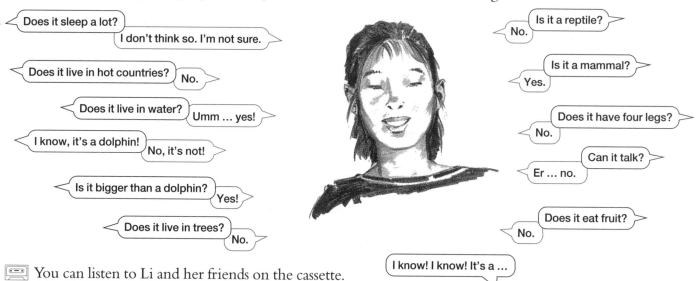

Does it sleep a lot?
I don't think so. I'm not sure.
Does it live in hot countries? No.
Does it live in water? Umm … yes!
I know, it's a dolphin! No, it's not!
Is it bigger than a dolphin? Yes!
Does it live in trees? No.

Is it a reptile? No.
Is it a mammal? Yes.
Does it have four legs? No.
Can it talk? Er … no.
Does it eat fruit? No.

I know! I know! It's a …

You can listen to Li and her friends on the cassette.

5 The natural world: a quiz

Present simple questions

Can you answer these questions? Ask your friends and family.
Next lesson, compare answers with other people in your class.

1 How many legs do spiders have?

2 What are cows: mammals or reptiles?

3 What is 'coral'? A plant, a stone, or an animal?

4 What do polar bears eat?

5 What is the fastest speed a bird can fly – 50 kph, 100 kph, 150 kph, or 200 kph?

6 How long does it take for a chicken to come from an egg – one week, two weeks, three weeks or four weeks?

6.1 The Venus flytrap

Read about a very strange plant.

CAN PLANTS EAT PEOPLE?

Can plants eat people? Probably not, but there are many plants that eat meat.
Some of them are big, and they can eat small animals.
One famous meat-eating plant is the Venus flytrap.

2 Why do they do it?

Most plants get energy from the sun, the air, and the ground. In some places, the ground is very poor. It doesn't have all the important things that plants need, especially nitrogen. Animal meat has a lot of nitrogen, so some plants eat meat to get what they need. Let's hope that some of the bigger plants don't get the same idea!

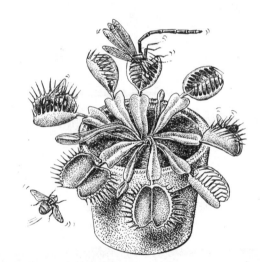

I A meat-eating plant

The Venus flytrap is a very strange plant. It grows in dry parts of the United States. Its leaves are like the pages of a book. They can open and close very quickly. Inside the leaves, there are three small hairs. If an insect touches one of the hairs, the leaf closes quickly. The insect cannot get out. In about half an hour, the leaf presses the insect until it is dead. Then, the plant covers the insect with a special liquid. Slowly, the plant eats the insect.

6.2 What are the questions?

Here is some information about Venus flytraps. What are the questions?

....   1 In the United States.

....   2 They look like the pages of a book.

....   3 Three small hairs.

....   4 Insects and small animals.

....   5 They need nitrogen.

7 Animals can talk

Personal pronouns

Choose the correct pronoun to complete the gap.

Language is very important for (*we/our/us*) .... With language, (*we/our/us*) .... can talk about different things. (*We/Our/Us*) .... can talk about the past, the present and the future. (*We/Our/Us*) .... are the only animals that have a language. Other animals can communicate but (*they/their/them*) .... can only say the same things.

For example, a young bird can tell (*it/its*) .... mother when (*it/its*) .... is hungry. Monkeys make noises when (*they/their/them*) .... are in danger. (*We/our/us*) .... can't understand (*they/their/them*) ...., but other monkeys know what the noises mean.

▭ Listen and check your answers.

The world of science

8 Goodbye, planet Earth!

Present continuous

It's three o'clock in the morning. High in the sky, over New York, there is a strange light in the sky. The television cameras are there. What is the reporter saying?

Write a sentence for each television picture.

1 I can see a bright light in the sky. It's moving. It's moving very fast.

2 ....

3 ....

4 ....

5 ....

6 ....

7 ....

8 ....

▭ You are the news reporter. Listen and tell the people what is happening.

9 What are the differences?

Comparatives

Here are two new spaceships. How is *Starlight* different from *Skywalker*? Write six sentences. You can use these words:

fast long strong heavy new expensive

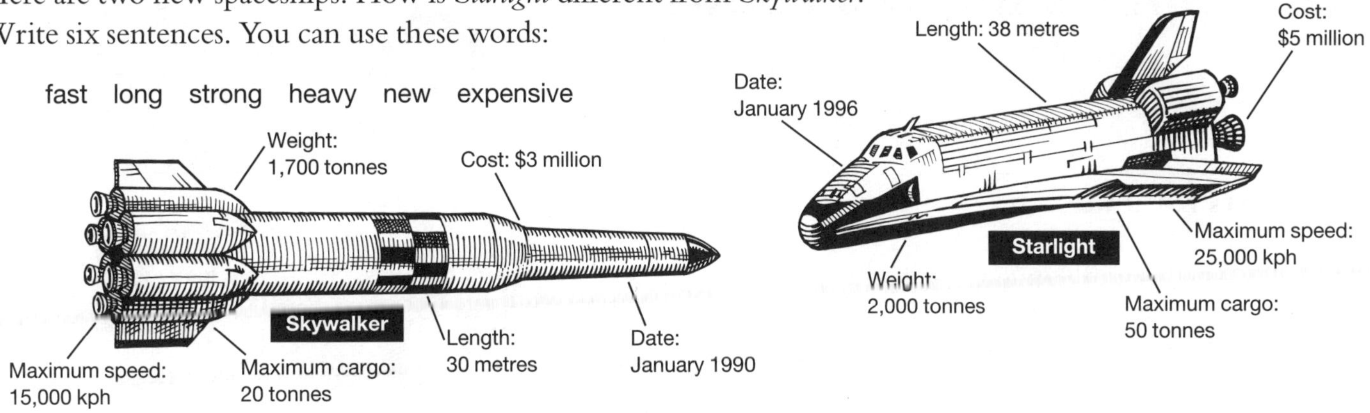

Weight:
1,700 tonnes
Cost: $3 million
Skywalker
Maximum speed:
15,000 kph
Maximum cargo:
20 tonnes
Length:
30 metres
Date:
January 1990
Length: 38 metres
Cost:
$5 million
Date:
January 1996
Starlight
Maximum speed:
25,000 kph
Weight:
2,000 tonnes
Maximum cargo:
50 tonnes

....

....

....

....

10 What do you know about space?

Comparatives; Present simple

Are these sentences right or wrong? If you don't know, find out. Look in books, or ask your family and friends.

If the sentence is wrong, put it right.

a The moon is hot.
Wrong! The moon is very cold.

b Mercury is the coldest planet, because it is very far from the sun.

....

c A year on Mercury is longer than a year on Earth.

....

d Pluto is the biggest planet.

....

e The sun and the moon are the same size.

....

f We know that there is life on Mars.

....

g The first person on the moon was a woman.

....

h The first woman in space was from Russia.

....

3 Topic Sports for everybody

1 Sports for Paul

Read about Paul and the sports that he does. Can you write the correct name of the day under each bag?

Paul loves sports. He does some sport every day. After school on Mondays, he goes running with some friends for about half an hour. Then he goes swimming before he goes home for dinner. He also plays in two school teams. On Wednesdays he plays football at school and on Friday evening he plays in the table tennis team. On Saturday and Sunday mornings he goes swimming again. He also cycles to school every day except Sunday. On Sunday afternoon, he does his favourite sport – sleeping!

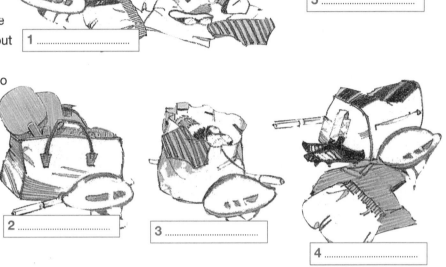

1 ....

2 ....

3 ....

4 ....

5 ....

2 What's the word?

Vocabulary

Write the correct word into the squares. What do they spell?

1 In anaerobic sports, you move s _ _ _ _ _ _ _.
2 Sports help to im_ _ _ _ _ your blood circulation.
3 A red liquid in your body.
4 Football makes your legs s _ _ _ _ _ .
5 Is swimming or football b _ _ _ _ _ for you?
6 If you want to lift very heavy things, you need strong m _ _ _ _ _ _.
7 Swimming is a good way to keep f _ _.
8 Do you e _ _ _ _ doing sports?
9 A pump in your body.
10 Very good.
11 In basketball, you have to m _ _ _ quickly.
12 H _ _ _! The house is on fire!
13 You don't need a lot of e _ _ _ _ _ to walk.
14 Some very old games that started in Greece.
15 Badminton can make your body f _ _ _ _ _ _ _.
16 We breathe it out. _ _ _.
17 What sports do you d_?
18 Exercise is good for your b _ _ _.

3 Talk to Peter

Writing and speaking

Write your answers to Peter's questions. Tell him what you think about sports.

PETER: Hello. How are you?

YOU: ....

PETER: I'm very tired. Today is my sports day. I go swimming in the morning and then I play football in the afternoon. Do you do any sports?

YOU: ....

PETER: Oh, really? I like sports a lot. My favourite sport is badminton. Do you have a favourite sport?

YOU: ....

PETER: I'm in the school badminton team. Are you in a team?

YOU: ....

PETER: In my school, people play football a lot. What sports do people play in your school?

YOU: ....

PETER: I like watching football on television. Do you like watching sports on television?

YOU: ....

PETER: That's interesting. Oh, look at the time! I've got a football game now. Bye!

You can talk to Peter on the cassette.

4 A game to play at school

Reading

Read about 'Rounders', a game that they play in England.

Match rules 1, 3, 5 and 6 on page 14 to the pictures.

ROUNDERS

'Rounders' is very popular in schools in England. The rules are very simple. You can play it with your friends.

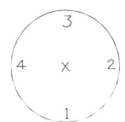

WHAT YOU NEED

A tennis ball, a stick, and something to mark five posts.

THIS IS HOW TO PLAY:

1 Make two teams, A and B, with about nine people in each team.

2 Mark four 'posts' in a circle on the ground, and one in the centre. You can use five coats, bags, books – anything. Place the posts like this:

3 A person from Team A stands at post 1 with a stick. A person from Team B stands in the middle and throws the ball to the person with the stick.

4 The person from Team A tries to hit the ball. Then, they run to the next post.

If they can run all the way round and back to post 1, then the team gets a point.

If they don't have time to run all the way round, they can stop at posts 2, 3 or 4.

5 While the person is running, Team B tries to get the ball and touch a post with it. If they do this, the person is 'out' and leaves the game. If they catch the ball when the person has hit it, the whole team is out.

6 Team B plays after Team A.

7 The winning team is the team with the most 'rounds' or points.

---

5 A day in your life

What do you do every day? Look at Unit 3, Exercise 7.2 in your Student's Book and write about a day in your life.

---

6 Say it clearly!

Be careful how you say 'ing'! Listen, and say the sentences.

/ɪŋ/

Swimming makes you flexible.
Walking is good for you.
Running is a good way to keep fit.
I like cycling, walking, swimming, running, sleeping and eating!

---

7 Sing a song! Sports for everybody

See page 154 in your Student's Book for the words to 'Sports for everybody'.

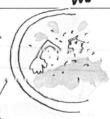

4 Language focus

1 What did he say?

Reading

Steve Johnson is an international tennis player. He talked to Jane Steinberg about his work. Choose the correct reply (a–d) for each of Jane's questions.

JANE: This year is an important year for you, isn't it, Steve?

STEVE: .... (1)

JANE: That's a lot of travelling!

STEVE: .... (2)

JANE: When did you start playing in international competitions?

STEVE: .... (3)

JANE: You have a very exciting life now, Steve.

STEVE: .... (4)

Steve's replies:

a A lot, yes, but I love travelling. I enjoy playing in different countries.

b When I was about 14. I played in Paris, and I won! But then I stopped playing for a few years. I had a lot of schoolwork.

c Exciting, yes, but it's a lot of hard work. If you want to stay at the top, you can't stop training, you know.

d Yes, that's right. In March I've an important game in Frankfurt. In June I'm in America, and in August I'm in Russia.

▭ You can check your answers with the cassette.

2 All about you

Verb + '-ing'

Think back to when you were younger. What did you like doing? What did you hate doing? When did you start doing something? When did you stop doing something? Write some sentences on the timeline.
For example:

When I was five, I started riding a bicycle.   When I was ..., I liked ... .
When I was ..., I stopped ... .   When I was ..., I hated ... .

	1 year old	3 years old	5 years old	8 years old	10 years old	
BIRTH						13 YEARS OLD

3 Talk to Sarah

Look at the posters. What type of films do you like?

An action film

A cartoon

A romantic film

A Western

A thriller

Now write your answers to Sarah's questions.

SARAH: What's your favourite type of film?

YOU: ....

SARAH: Why do you think that?

YOU: ....

SARAH: Do you like historical films?

YOU: ....

SARAH: Well, I don't like them. I think they're boring. What's the name of your favourite film at the moment?

YOU: ....

SARAH: Can you tell me what it's about?

YOU: ....

SARAH: How does it finish?

YOU: ....

SARAH: Sounds great! I'd like to see it!

You can talk to Sarah on the cassette.

4 How do they do it?

Adverbs

Write a sentence about each picture. Use the adjective to make an adverb.

1 loud
2 happy
3 quiet
4 hard
5 slow
6 fast
7 dangerous

7 D A N G E R O U S L Y

Now write the adverbs in the correct squares.

5 What can you say?

Classroom phrases

What can you say in your English lesson, in these situations?

a You haven't got a pen. ....

b You can't find the right page in your book. ....

c You can't hear your teacher. ....

d You need more time to finish the exercise. ....

e You want your teacher to check your work. ....

6 Say it clearly!

/liː/, /ɪliː/

Look at the adverbs in Exercise 4. Can you say them clearly?

Listen to the cassette and say the words.

dangerously loudly quietly slowly
happily easily angrily noisily

a

b

c

d

5 Fluency practice A good life – for you!

1   What do you think?

What things do you think are important for 'a good life'? Tick the box with your
answer (√). Add three more things to the list and tick your answer.

	very important				not very important
1 a lot of friends	☐	☐	☐	☐	☐
2 long school holidays	☐	☐	☐	☐	☐
3 a lot of things to do outside the house	☐	☐	☐	☐	☐
4 a lot of things to do inside the house	☐	☐	☐	☐	☐
5 time to watch television	☐	☐	☐	☐	☐
6 trips to other places or countries	☐	☐	☐	☐	☐
7 a lot of interesting books to read	☐	☐	☐	☐	☐
8 more lessons after school	☐	☐	☐	☐	☐
9 doing sports	☐	☐	☐	☐	☐
10	☐	☐	☐	☐	☐
11	☐	☐	☐	☐	☐
12	☐	☐	☐	☐	☐

Next lesson, compare your answers with other students in your class.

2   Things you like

What do you like? What don't you like? Make two idea maps.

Things I like

Things I don't like

Now write about each idea map. Say something more about each thing on your idea
map. For example:

The things I like
I like playing football a lot. After school, I usually play with my
friends in the park. It's great fun. I also like making things. I like
making models of cars and houses. I have lots of models at home.
Sometimes I paint them.

6 Help yourself with vocabulary

In Level 1, there were two ways to help you learn vocabulary.
You can see them again in this Unit, and you can also see another way.
Use them to learn the words in this Theme (Units 3–7).

From Level 1

1 Make a word bag

If you put the new words on pieces of paper in a bag, you can test yourself.

1 Copy the new words onto cards.

2 Write the meaning
in your language,
or draw a picture.

3 Put the cards in a bag.

4 Take one out and
test yourself!

heart

You try it! Make cards with the words from your *Language Record*. Put them in a bag
and test yourself.

2 Make a jigsaw

1 Copy a paragraph from your book.

2 Cut out some words.

A DAY IN THE LIFE OF SUSAN SPENCER
Susan Spencer, just 14 years old is one
of England's top swimmers. Susan
wants to swim for England in the Olympics
and win a gold medal. Susan's life is
probably very different from yours.

Her day starts at 4.00am, when
she gets up and begins training. She
has the same timetable every day. She
swims 400 lengths (20 kilometres)
and still has time for school
work.

3 Mix them up.

4 Put the words in the right place.

Check your answers, and do it again!

Now try it for yourself. Copy a text from Theme A (Units 3-7) of your Student's Book.

Another way to help you learn vocabulary

3 Make a crossword

Make a list of the new words in a Unit. Make a crossword with them.

For example:

strong   need   flexible   enjoy   health

heart   lungs   excellent   muscles

```
                        H
          MUSCLES       E
   F             T      A
   L             R      R
   E     N       O      T
EXCELLENT        N
   I     E       G
   B     E
   L     D
   HEALTH
         U
         N
         G
         S
```

Write the meaning in your language beside each word.

Look at Units 3-7 in your Student's Book and make a list of some words. Make your crossword. Check the meaning of each word in your dictionary.

Use the 'Three ways to learn vocabulary' above to learn the words in the next Units that you do.

7 Test yourself

Here are some things you learned to do in Units 3-6. How well can you do them? Put a tick (√) in the box.

I can do it:	very well	OK	a little
1 Talk about sports.			
2 Ask about daily routines.			
3 Talk about daily routines.			
4 Talk about likes and dislikes.			

1 Play basketball

Talk about sports

Look at this information about basketball.

| | Energy level | Does it make you: | |
		strong?	flexible?
Basketball	3	√√√	√√

Read the texts on page 25 in your Student's Book again and write a short paragraph about basketball. Say:

how it is good for you   how much energy you need
who can do it   what you need to play it

....

....

....

....

2 School in England

Ask about daily routines

You want to ask an English student about school in England. What can you ask? Write five questions. Some ideas:

subjects   times   meals at school   uniform   after school
numbers of students in the class

....

....

....

....

3 A strange life

Read and write about daily routines

Read about what Bill does every day.

Bill starts the day at half-past seven in the morning. He gets up, gets dressed and then he goes straight out to work. He leaves the house at about eight o'clock. He cycles to work and it takes about half an hour. He works in a toothpaste factory. He puts the tops on the tubes. He stays there until lunchtime at one o'clock, when he goes home again. He's at home for three hours and then he goes back to work. He works in a different place in the afternoon. He trains lions in the zoo. He works there for about four hours and then he goes to his next job. He cycles there, but it only takes a quarter of an hour. He tests beds in a bed factory. He finishes work at about eleven o'clock. Bill says: 'I like living dangerously, but not all the time!'

Write the time when Bill does each thing.

7:30 Bill gets up

4 What do they like doing?

Express likes and dislikes

Look at the pictures. What do these people like doing? What don't they like doing? Write a sentence about each one.

like   love   hate

A picture dictionary (1)

Label the picture.

body

h...................................

h...................................

l...................................

a...................................

b...................................

h...................................

m...................................

l...................................

f...................................

What's the verb?

keep fit

br...................................

wi...................................

im...................................

What's the adjective?

flexible

st...................................

li...................................

ex...................................

What's the adverb?

fast

sl...................................

da...................................

ha...................................

qu...................................

su...................................

8 Topic In a rainforest

1 What's the word?

Vocabulary

Join the parts of the word. Match them to the pictures.

rept	fru	ri	wor	rub	medi	ra	pla	in	for

est	cine	sect	in	ile	nt	ce	it	ber	ld

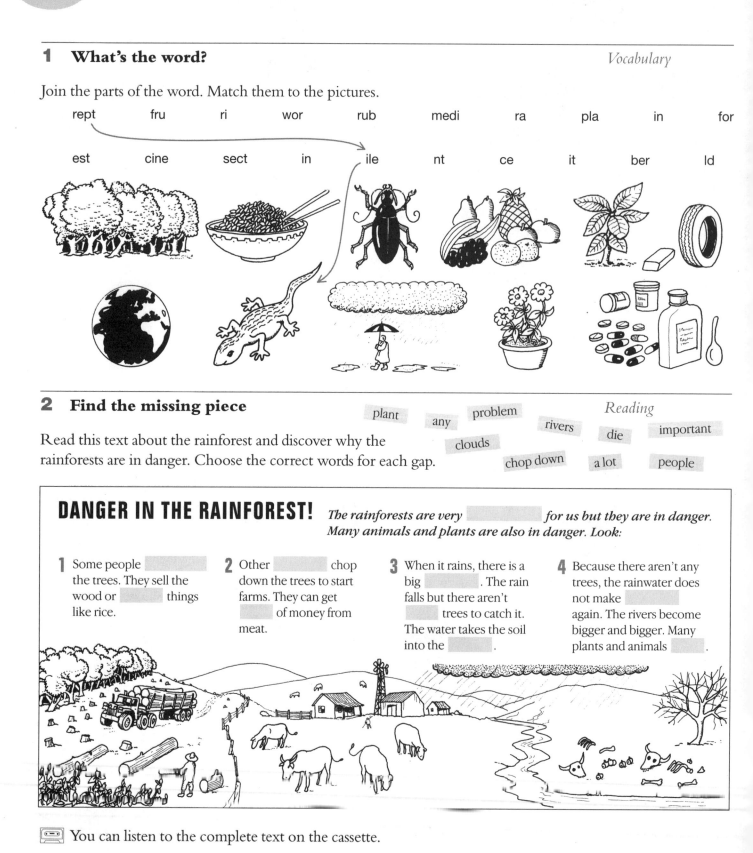

2 Find the missing piece

Reading

Read this text about the rainforest and discover why the rainforests are in danger. Choose the correct words for each gap.

plant   any   problem   rivers   die   important   clouds   chop down   a lot   people

DANGER IN THE RAINFOREST!

The rainforests are very _____ for us but they are in danger. Many animals and plants are also in danger. Look:

1 Some people _____ the trees. They sell the wood or _____ things like rice.

2 Other _____ chop down the trees to start farms. They can get _____ of money from meat.

3 When it rains, there is a big _____. The rain falls but there aren't _____ trees to catch it. The water takes the soil into the _____.

4 Because there aren't any trees, the rainwater does not make _____ again. The rivers become bigger and bigger. Many plants and animals _____.

🔲 You can listen to the complete text on the cassette.

3 Sing a song! Mother forest

See page 154 in your Student's Book
for the words to 'Mother forest'.

---

4 Talk to Peter

Speaking

Write your answers to Peter's questions. Tell him about the countryside in
your country.

PETER: Hello. How are you?

YOU: ....

PETER: I feel great! Yesterday, I went to my uncle's farm. He's got hundreds
of cows. Are there any farms near you?

YOU: ....

PETER: What do they have on farms in your country?

YOU: ....

PETER: That's interesting. Near my uncle's farm there's a big forest. Are there
any forests near you?

YOU: ....

PETER: In the forest near my uncle's farm, there are lots of wild animals and
birds. What wild animals do you have in your country?

YOU: ....

PETER: Oh, really! Are there any rainforests in your country?

YOU: ....

PETER: There aren't any rainforests in my country. I live in England and it's
too cold. What's the weather like in your country?

YOU: ....

PETER: Is it the same all the time?

YOU: ....

PETER: I'd like to visit your country sometime. Anyway, I have to go now.
Talk to you later. Bye!

YOU: ....

You can talk to Peter on the cassette.

Trees give us information about the past. Read about what they can tell us.

Secrets from the trees

Trees give us many things. They give us wood, oxygen, rubber, medicines and many other things. They can also tell us a lot, too. How?

If you cut across a tree, you can see that it has 'rings'. Most trees grow one new ring every year. Because of this we know how old a tree is. The Bristlecone Pines in California are over 4,000 years old. This means that they have over 4,000 rings.

When the climate is dry or very cold, trees do not grow very much and their rings are usually thin. When it is wet and good for trees, the rings are much thicker. If the rings are suddenly very thin or suddenly much thicker, this means that the climate changed suddenly. If we look at the rings on the Bristlecone Pines we can learn about the climate 4,000 years ago. We can see how our climate is changing today.

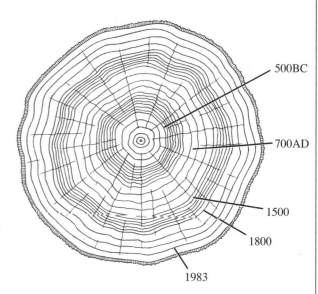

Answer these questions:

1 Look at the tree rings in the picture. How was the weather between 1500 and 1800?

2 If a tree has very thick rings, what does it mean?

3 Scientists say the Earth is warmer and wetter now. How do you think tree rings look today?

6 Say it clearly!   /e/ *and* /aː/

6.1 /e/

🔲 Smile and say /e/

help   insect   reptile   many   medicine   very   wet

6.2 /aː/

🔲 Open your mouth and say /aː/

dark   part   plant   are   aren't   large

Help! There are reptiles and insects in my medicine!

It's part of a large, dark plant.

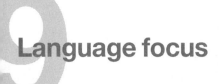

Language focus

1 Learn more about dinosaurs

Reading

Read about the dinosaurs and then look at the picture. Can you find seven mistakes in the picture?

Did dinosaurs live together?
Some types of dinosaurs lived in small groups. We know this because many dinosaur bones are in the same place.

Did people live at the same time as dinosaurs?
No! The last dinosaur disappeared about 65 million years ago. The first people appeared about 150,000 years ago.

Did dinosaurs sleep in the winter?
Probably not. Today, animals sleep in the winter because it is cold. Millions of years ago, it was always hot.

Were dinosaurs mammals?
No. There weren't any mammals on earth at the time of the dinosaurs. Dinosaurs were reptiles. They laid eggs and they had cold blood. They did not give milk to their babies.

Did dinosaurs fly?
No! All dinosaurs lived on land.

How fast were dinosaurs?
Some dinosaurs moved very slowly but other dinosaurs moved very quickly.

Did dinosaurs live in the sea?
No. Dinosaurs lived on land. Sometimes they went into water for a short time, but they did not live in water.

What was the biggest dinosaur?
The biggest dinosaur was probably the *Seismosaurus*. It was over 35 metres long. It was heavier than nine African elephants.

What did dinosaurs eat?
Most dinosaurs were plant-eaters. The *Apatosaurus*, for example, had a long, thin neck so that it could eat leaves from trees. Other dinosaurs were meat-eaters. The *Tyrannosaurus Rex*, for example, killed smaller dinosaurs for food.

2 Fill the gaps

'was' and 'were'

Write 'was' or 'were' in each space.

Millions of years ago, there .... many types of dinosaurs on Earth.
Some dinosaurs .... meat-eaters and other dinosaurs .... plant-eaters.
The biggest meat-eating dinosaur .... probably the
Tyrannosaurus Rex. It .... about as long as four cars and as
tall as the tallest giraffe today. Its head .... about 1.2 metres long.
Its teeth .... very sharp. Its legs
.... very big but it .... too heavy
to run for a long time. It killed other
dinosaurs for food.

The smallest dinosaur .... also a meat-eater. It .... the *Compsognathus*.
It .... only 50 cm long. It walked on two legs and it had many sharp teeth.

3 What's the answer?

Past simple with regular verbs

Look at the information in Exercises 1 and 2, and on page 50 in your Student's
Book. Write your answers to these questions.

a When did the dinosaurs die? They died...

b When did people appear on Earth? People appeared.......................

c Did dinosaurs live on the land or in the sea? They lived...............

d Did dinosaurs live together or alone? ....

e Did dinosaurs walk on two legs or four legs? ....

f Where did scientists discover the first dinosaur bones? ....

g Did dinosaurs kill other dinosaurs? Yes, Tyrannosaurus Rex........

h Did the *Tyrannosaurus Rex* look friendly? ....

4 What happened to the dinosaurs?

Past simple with regular verbs

Read about how the dinosaurs disappeared. Fill the gaps with the correct past form
of the verb ('-ed') or 'was/were'.

Scientists are not sure why the dinosaurs ....
(disappear). Some scientists think that the climate
.... (change) suddenly. Fossils of trees tell us
that the temperature .... (drop) a lot and
that the level of the sea .... (drop) also.
This means that it .... (was/were) suddenly much
colder. Perhaps the dinosaurs .... (was/were) too
slow to change with the climate.
A new idea is that a meteor .... (crash) into
the Earth. Scientists .... (discover) a place in

Mexico where they think the meteor ....
(crash). They think that there .... (was/were) a lot
of dust from the meteor. The dust .... (land)
on the plants. Many animals – including some
dinosaurs – .... (was/were) plant-eaters, and
perhaps the dust .... (kill) them. This means that
there .... (was/were) nothing for meat-eating
dinosaurs to eat, and so they .... (die). But, as
many animals from that time didn't die, we are not
100% sure what really .... (happen).

5 Say it clearly!

There are three ways of saying '–ed' in English:

a 't' sound (/t/), for example: look**ed**
an 'id' sound (/ɪd/) , for example: visit**ed**
a 'd' sound (/d/), for example: stay**ed**

Listen. Say the verbs.

liked wanted decided asked stayed visited
changed studied looked watched played
discovered dropped climbed happened landed

Put the verbs in the columns.
Check your answers with the cassette.

looked /t/	visited /ɪd/	stayed /d/

6 Talk to Sarah

Inviting and suggesting

Write your answers to Sarah's questions.

SARAH: Hello! What are you doing?

YOU: ....

SARAH: That's interesting. What are you doing later?

YOU: ....

SARAH: I've got a swimming lesson later. Do you like swimming?

YOU: ....

SARAH: Why don't you come swimming with me one day? It's good for you!

YOU: ....

SARAH: Let's talk about it again later. Listen! Do you like singing?

YOU: ....

SARAH: I like singing a lot. Do you know any songs in English?

YOU: ....

SARAH: Oh, I don't know that song. Why don't you sing it to me now?

YOU: ....

SARAH: Beautiful! Look, there's a song in Unit 8 of the Student's Book. Let's
sing it now!

You can talk to Sarah on the cassette.

Fluency practice   More poems from the rainforest

1 Some poems to read

Read these poems. Do you think the writer is happy or sad?

* I am a bird in the rainforest. I live in the rainforest, high in the trees. I can see the clouds above me. It's hot here, very hot, but the rain makes me cool. I can fly from tree to tree. There's so much life in the forest. It's so good to be here.

* I am a flower in the rainforest. Millions of years ago, dinosaurs walked on this land. Millions of years ago plants were tall and big. Millions of years ago it was hot, hot. Under my feet are the bones of dinosaurs. Where did they go? Now I am in the rainforest, it's dark. The ground is wet. It's hot and I'm afraid. I don't like it. The light is coming. Where can I go?

2 Write a poem

Imagine you are something in the rainforest. How do you feel? What are you thinking? What can you see? Write a poem. You can listen to the tape while you think. There is music from South America on it.

I am a cloud

I am an insect

I am a humming bird

I am a tree

I am a frog

You can use these ideas.

I can hear the rain   It's hot, dark and wet in the rainforest.
I can hear the sounds of animals.   I can see the sky.
The wind is warm and wet.   I live here in the dark, wet forest.

11 Help yourself with writing

Two ways to help yourself with writing

1   An experiment

There are two main ways to write. Try an experiment.

1.1 Fast then slowly
Write fast! Then go slowly.
Choose a topic from the box (or some other topic).
Write as much as you can in 10 minutes.

dinosaurs   my favourite sport   trees   animals   my house   my school   America   my town   things I like

After 10 minutes, take another 10 minutes to check your work carefully.

1.2 Slowly and carefully
Write slowly and carefully.
Choose another topic from the box. Work for 20 minutes. Write slowly and
carefully. Only write what you know is correct.

Look at your work. Which is better for you: 'fast then slowly', or 'slowly and carefully'?

2   Make a list of your mistakes

2.1 What's wrong?
Look at these sentences. There is a mistake in each sentence. What is it?
(You can check your answers on page 96.)

Dinosaurs livved millions of years ago.

Yesterday, I play football.

What's the time.

Sophie go to school with Barbara.

I sitting on a chair.

My brother has got a car biy.

2.2 Your mistakes
Look at your work in English. What mistakes do you make?
Make a list of six mistakes that you often make. For example:

1 Spelling: sport, pos/ible   4

2 'be': am/is/are — don't forget!   5

3 Word order: a big car   6

Help yourself! Use your list to check your work in future.

12 Revision Under a volcano

1 What's the word?

Vocabulary

Read these clues. Can you find the word in the forest?

a An animal that flies.

b We take this when we are ill.

c The part of a plant under the ground.

d Snakes and frogs are r........................ .

e An animal that has six legs.

f In the rainforest it is always w.................. .

g Rain comes from ....

h The Wollemi Pines started growing when
d........................ lived in Australia.

i Nobody knows for sure why the dinosaurs suddenly
dis.................. .

j Tyrannosaurus Rex was a ....-eater.

k In Java, the people wanted to ch........................
the trees to grow ....

2 Talk to Peter

Speaking; Past simple

Write your answers to Peter's questions. Tell him what you know about dinosaurs.

PETER: Hello. How are you?

YOU: ....

PETER: Can you help me with my homework? Do you know anything about
dinosaurs?

YOU: ....

PETER: Great! Now, my first question is: were there people on earth at the
same time as dinosaurs?

YOU: ....

PETER: Oh, really? When did the dinosaurs disappear?

YOU: ....

PETER: That long ago! Do scientists know why dinosaurs disappeared? Something about a meteor, I think.

YOU: ....

PETER: Yes, that's right! Next question. Did dinosaurs all walk on four legs?

YOU: ....

PETER: Were all the dinosaurs very big?

YOU: ....

PETER: Oh, that's interesting! You certainly know a lot about dinosaurs! My last question is: how do you spell 'dinosaur'?

YOU: ....

PETER: Thanks very much! Talk to you later. Bye.

YOU: ....

🎞 Now talk to Peter on the cassette.

---

3 Another Wonder of the World: volcanoes

Reading

What do you know about volcanoes? Are these sentences true [T] or false [F]?

1 Volcanoes come from mountains. ☐
2 Volcanoes are only in the southern hemisphere of the world. ☐
3 There aren't any active volcanoes today. ☐
4 There aren't any volcanoes under the sea. ☐

Now read and check your answers.

What is a volcano?

UNDER THE GROUND, there are hot gases and liquid rock. Sometimes, these gases and rock explode out of the ground. The liquid rock is called lava. When it becomes colder it becomes very hard. Slowly, as more and more lava comes out, it makes a big hill.

Many of the world's volcanoes are in the Pacific Ocean, but there are also volcanoes in Japan, Mexico, Italy, Turkey and many other countries. There are about 500 active volcanoes in the world today; many of them are under the sea.

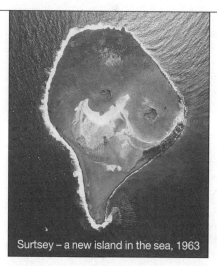
Surtsey – a new island in the sea, 1963

In 1963, a new island appeared in the sea. A volcano under the sea pushed lava up to the surface near Iceland. Today, the island, called Surtsey, has plants and flowers on it.

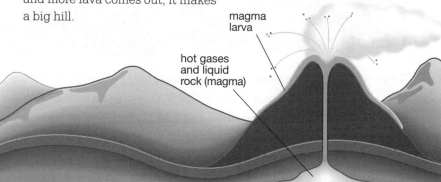

magma
larva

hot gases
and liquid
rock (magma)

4 Two famous volcanoes

4.1 Paricutin and San Juan

Read about when the volcano Paricutin appeared.
Write the correct forms of the verbs (1–15).

Paricutin is a new volcano. It is active today. One day in 1943, a farmer ....(1)........ (was/were) in his fields. He ....(2)........ (was/were) surprised to see steam coming from the ground. Suddenly, the land ....(3)........ (open) and lava ....(4)........ (start) to come out. The farmer ....(5)........ (hurry) back to his village to tell everyone. They ....(6)........ (was/were) very frightened. After a few hours, there ....(7)........ (was/were) already a small mountain of lava. Next morning, it ....(8)........ (was/were) over 15 metres high. About 500 people ....(9)........ (live) in the town of San Juan near there. They ....(10)........ (decide) to leave and they ....(11)........ (move) to another town. They ....(12)........ (was/were) very lucky because, two weeks later, the lava ....(13)........ (cover) San Juan. Paricutin ....(14)........ (stop) producing lava in 1952, when it ....(15)........ (was/were) 425 metres high. Today, the church tower is the only thing you can see in San Juan.

4.2 Vesuvius and Pompeii

Can you complete the sentences (1–6) with the phrases in the volcano?

On 24 August 79AD, the volcano Vesuvius in Italy suddenly erupted. The lava and thick clouds of dust travelled for many kilometres.

Dust from the volcano covered the bodies of the people in Pompeii

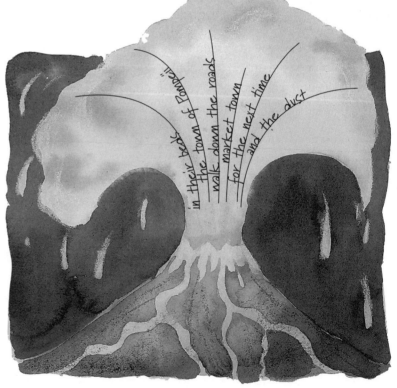

in their beds
the town of Pompeii
walk down the roads
market town
for the next time
and the dust

Pompeii was a rich ....(1)........ near Vesuvius. In the town, many people were still ....(2)......... They tried to escape, but over 2,000 people died. The lava, the heat, ...(3)........ killed them. The dust covered their bodies. Today, you can see exactly what they were doing when they died. You can walk around ....(4)......... You can go inside the houses and you can ....(5)......... Vesuvius is still active. The last time it erupted was in 1944. People are waiting ....(6).........

A picture dictionary (2)

Label the picture.

c_____
b_____
s_____
i_____
tree_____
w_____
l_____
f_____
r_____
g_____
p_____
r_____
f_____

What's the adjective?

What's the past tense of the verb?

tall_____
d_____
h_____
w_____
la_____

chopped down
d_____
cr_____
st_____
w_____
l_____
pl_____
dis_____
cli_____

---

1 Inventions and discoveries

Vocabulary

1.1 A puzzle

How many world inventions can you find in this puzzle?
Write the words by the pictures.

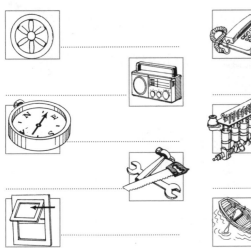

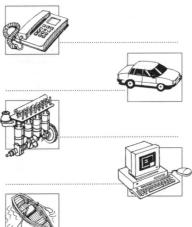

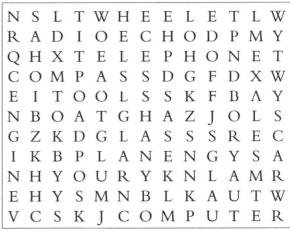

```
N S L T W H E E L E T L W
R A D I O E C H O D P M Y
Q H X T E L E P H O N E T
C O M P A S S D G F D X W
E I T O O L S S K F B A Y
N B O A T G H A Z J O L S
G Z K D G L A S S R E C
I K B P L A N E N G Y S A
N H Y O U R Y K N L A M R
E H Y S M N B L K A U T W
V C S K J C O M P U T E R
```

1.2 Make your own puzzle

Make a word puzzle like this for your friends to do.

---

2 Life in Egypt 4,000 years ago

*Reading; listening;
Past simple verb forms*

2.1 Dr Wilson talks about Egypt

In Europe 4,000 years ago people lived in simple houses and used simple tools.
At that time, Egypt was much more advanced than Europe. Dr Wilson, an
archaeologist, is talking to Stephen Thornton about life in Egypt 4,000 years ago.

Read the dialogue and put the pictures in order (1–5).

Life in Egypt was very different from
life in Europe 4,000 years ago.

DR WILSON:	Life in Egypt was very different from life in Europe 4,000 years ago.
STEPHEN THORNTON:	How?
DR WILSON:	Well, I have some pictures here. You can see that the Egyptians built some very big buildings. The pyramids, for example.
STEPHEN THORNTON:	Are they really 4,000 years old?
DR WILSON:	Yes! They tell us a lot about life in Egypt.
STEPHEN THORNTON:	What do they tell us?
DR WILSON:	Well, we discovered jewellery in the pyramids. We know the Egyptians went to other countries to buy the stones. You can see one of their boats in this picture.
STEPHEN THORNTON:	Mm. Did they sell things?
DR WILSON:	Food and wine, I think.
STEPHEN THORNTON:	That's very interesting. Did they write?
DR WILSON:	Yes, archaeologists found old paper called papyrus in the pyramids.
STEPHEN THORNTON:	What did they eat?
DR WILSON:	Well, we found some bread in the pyramids, so we know they ate corn. We think they were good farmers … and soldiers.
STEPHEN THORNTON:	Did they fight wars?
DR WILSON:	Oh, yes. They had lots of wars … .

You can listen to the dialogue on the cassette.

2.2 Check your understanding

Read the dialogue and answer the questions. Use these verbs in the Past simple:

go – went   build – built   eat – ate   find – found   be – was/were   discover – discovered

1 Did the Egyptians travel?

   Yes, they went ....

2 What did they eat?

   They ate ....

3 What did they build?

   They ....

4 What did the archaeologists find in the pyramids?

   They ....

5 What jobs did the Egyptians do?

   They ....

6 Where did the archaeologists discover Egyptian bread?

   They ....

3 The detectives of history

Archaeologists find a clue.

> We know that the Egyptians had corn

Deducing

So they make a guess.

> … so they probably made bread.

Then they ask a question.

> But how did they make bread?

Look at the clues, guesses and questions here. Which ones go together?

The Egyptians brought stones for jewellery from different countries …	So they probably believed in a new life after death.	But what food did they grow?
The Egyptians put food in the pyramids …	So they were probably farmers.	But what did they write with?
The Egyptians had writing …	So they probably travelled.	But which countries did they visit?
We know the land by the river Nile was very good …	So they probably had documents.	But what other things did they believe in?

4 Say it clearly!

/ɔː/ *four, more*

4.1 Listen and say the words

Four or more?

Many words in English have the same sound as 'four' and 'more'. Listen. Say the sentences and words.

My cat has four paws.   I saw four poor men at the door.

four paw poor door saw bought more before for or

4.2 Different letter patterns

How many different ways to spell /ɔː/ are there? Make a list and write the words.

OR: for, or …
OUR: our …

PAWS

5 Sing a song! Pyramids and dinosaurs (a long, long, long time ago)

See page 155 in your Student's Book for the words to 'Pyramids and dinosaurs (a long, long, long time ago)'.

14 Language focus

Revision of Past simple:
regular and irregular
forms; reacting

1 Two true, accidental discoveries

Reading

1.1 The Dead Sea Scrolls

In 1947, some boys discovered some very important papers. Read their story.

A scroll = a piece of paper like this:

How they discovered the Dead Sea Scrolls

One day, about 50 years ago in a village near the Dead Sea, some boys decided to play a game together. They went out of the village to find some trees. One of them saw a cave and they went into it.

One boy waited outside and began to count: 'One, two, three, … eighteen, nineteen, twenty … I'm coming!' He went into the cave to look for his friends.

'I think they are behind the wall,' he said. He climbed the wall of the cave and suddenly a stone fell from the wall. In the wall he saw some big pots.

'Look boys! Come here! Look at this!' he shouted. His friends came to see. They got the pots out of the hole in the wall and put them on the ground. 'Let's open the pots!' one of the boys said. In the pots, they found some very old pieces of paper with strange writing on them. 'Let's go and tell our teacher about this,' another boy said.
The boys went to find their teacher in Qumran, their village. He told them that the papers were probably 2,000 years old.

Now put a number beside each picture, to tell the story.

1.2 Find the verbs

Find the past tense of these verbs in the story.

get .... go .... see .... begin .... fall .... come .... find .... tell ....

What is the boy saying? Fill the gap with correct verb in the past tense.

1 We .... to play out of the village.

2 My friends .... into a big cave.

3 I .... to find them. I climbed up a wall and some stones .... out of the wall.

7 We .... to tell you about the pots.

4 I .... something in the wall.

5 We .... the pots down from the wall.

6 In the pots, we .... some old papers.

1.3 Another cave, in France

Writing

Look at the pictures and write the story.

You can start like this:

Four boys, Jacques, Simon, Georges and Marcel, were friends.
In the summer of 1940 the weather was very hot. One day,...

....

....

....

....

....

....

....

2 Choose the question

2.1 Reporter's questions

A newspaper reporter asked the boys who found
the Dead Sea Scrolls some questions. Read their
answers and choose the correct question.

REPORTER: ....(1).......................

ANSWER: On Saturday afternoon.

REPORTER: ....(2).......................

ANSWER: We went to play hide and seek.

REPORTER: ....(3).......................

ANSWER: They were in some pots in the wall.

REPORTER: ....(4).......................

ANSWER: I climbed the wall and a stone fell out.

REPORTER: ....(5).......................

ANSWER: There was a lot of strange writing on the scrolls.

Reporter's questions

Why did you go in the cave?
When did you find the scrolls?
Where did you find the scrolls?
What did you see on the scrolls?
How did you find them?

2.2 Your questions

Write five questions you can ask the boys who found the cave paintings.

Where ...? ....

When ...? ....

How ...? ....

What ...? ....

Why ...? ....

3 True or false?

Read these sentences about you. If the sentence is false, put it right underneath, like this:

You were born in New York.
No, I wasn't. I was born in ... .

1 You went to Greenland on holiday last year.

No, I didn't ....

2 You bought an ice-cream yesterday.

....

3 You went to the cinema last week.

....

4 You ate fish yesterday for dinner.

....

5 You drank a glass of milk for breakfast this morning.

....

4 Talk to Sarah

You can use these words and phrases to talk to Sarah:

Oh, brilliant!   You lucky thing!   Oh, no!   Oh, bad luck!   That's terrible.

SARAH: Hi! Did you have a good weekend?

YOU: ....

SARAH: What did you do?

YOU: ....

SARAH: Oh! Well … my uncle took me for a ride in a plane!

YOU: ....

SARAH: Yes, it was great but …

YOU: ....

SARAH: After half an hour, I felt ill.

YOU: ....

SARAH: The plane landed, and I went home to bed. I was in bed all day yesterday.

YOU: ....

SARAH: I missed a Maths test at school!

YOU: ....

📼 You can talk to Sarah on the cassette.

---

5 Say it clearly!

5.1 He came and made a cake …

📼 All these words have the same long 'a' sound. Listen and repeat.

made came cake late wait
He came and made a cake.
Don't be late. I can't wait!

5.2 My fat cat is happy

📼 All these words have the same short 'a' sound. Listen and repeat.

sad bad band began happy angry
fat catch land axe
I feel sad, but my fat cat is happy.

Fluency practice An Iron-Age village

1 An accidental discovery in Glastonbury

Reading

Glastonbury is a small town in England.
Read about how they discovered an Iron-Age village there.

AN IRON-AGE VILLAGE IN GLASTONBURY

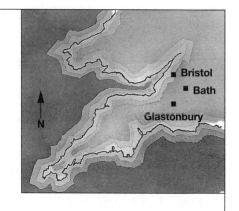

About 100 years ago, in 1895, there was a farmer called Stephen Laver. Mr Laver decided to make a new fence around his land. He made some deep holes in the ground. In one of the holes he found some strange things. They were pieces of old pots. He showed them to the school teacher in Glastonbury.

The teacher wrote a letter to Dr Bulleid, a famous archaeologist. She told him about the pots. He was very interested and he decided to go to Glastonbury. When he saw the pots and the other pieces he was very excited. He was sure that they were over 3,000 years old.

In 1908, Dr Bulleid started digging in Mr Laver's field. After a short time he discovered many more pots, iron tools, and bronze pots and jewellery. Then, one morning, he found the most exciting thing: a boat that was 3,000 years old! Dr Bulleid was right; 3,000 years ago there was a village in Glastonbury. The village was a special village, a 'lake village', where people lived on the water and went fishing.

Now put these pictures in the correct order to tell the story.
Write a number (1–6) in the boxes.

2 What's the answer?

Write your answers to these questions.

1 How many people are in the story?

....

2 Why was Dr Bulleid excited?

....

3 Why did these Iron-Age people have boats?

....

Write three more questions about the story for another student in your class.

....

....

....

3 Working with Dr Bulleid

Dr Bulleid and his team found many more Iron-Age things. Here are some of the things they found.

pot

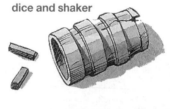

dice and shaker

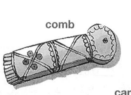

comb

ladle

wooden bowl

canoe

Imagine that it is 1908. You are working with Dr Bulleid. Write a letter to a friend. Tell him or her about the things you found.

Glastonbury
Somerset
England

20th August 1908

Dear
I am spending the holiday with Dr. Bulleid at Glastonbury Lake Village. It is ....
Every morning we .... Last week, we found .... Dr. Bulleid says ....
What are you doing this summer?

Write soon.
Best wishes

16 Help yourself with pronunciation

In Level 1, you saw three ways to help you learn pronunciation.
You can see them again in this Unit, and see one more way.
Use them to practise the words in this Theme (Units 13–15).

From Level 1

1 Listen, look and repeat

Using a mirror

You try it! Listen. Look in a mirror and say the words and phrases.

They ...

1 They lived in long houses.
   houses   long houses   in long houses   lived   they lived   they lived in
   They lived in long houses.
2 They didn't have horses, cats or chickens.
   chickens   cats or chickens   horses   have   didn't have
   They didn't have horses, cats or chickens.

2 Bang on the table!

*Stress in
three-syllable words*

2.1 Strong syllables

Here are some words with three syllables. In these words, the first syllable is the
strongest.

VEGetable   **BRILL**iant   **BEAU**tiful

In these words, the second syllable is the strongest.

de**TEC**tive   dis**COV**er   im**POR**tant

Say the words and bang your hand on the table when you say the strong syllable.

2.2 Listen and say the words

Listen and say the words. Don't forget to bang the desk on the stressed syllable!

VEGetable   **BRILL**iant   **BEAU**tiful   **PROB**ably   **MEX**ico   **HOS**pital
de**TEC**tive   dis**COV**er   im**POR**tant   ex**CIT**ing   com**PU**ter   pol**ICE**man

3 What are the important words?

3.1 Important words

In English, the important words are the strongest. Like this:

ALISON: Yes , thanks. I had a (great) time.
HELEN: (What) did you (do)?
ALISON: I went to the (beach) with Nick.

🖭 Listen. Say the dialogue.

3.2 A dialogue in your Student's Book

Find a dialogue in the Student's Book.
Put a circle around the important words.

OUT AND ABOUT!
NICK: The Mash Boys! They're (terrible!) I (hate) them! Just a lot of noise!
ALISON: All right, Nick. You're (not) going to the concert. What are you doing later, Will?
WILL: Nothing. Why don't we meet at my (house?)
ALISON: (Good) idea. Shall I tell Helen?
WILL: Fine. Let's meet at around (five.)
NICK: Tell Helen (not) to bring any Mash Boys records with her.
ALISON: Oh, be (quiet) Nick! See you later, Will. Bye!
WILL: Bye!

Say the dialogue. Say the words in the circles strongly.

A new way

4 Pretend you are another person

If you take two parts in a conversation in English, you can use a different voice for one of them.

Hi! How are you?

Hello, Peter. Fine, thanks.

I had a big surprise today.

Really, Peter! What was that?

You try it! Choose one of the dialogues with Peter or Sarah. Take both parts.
🖭 You can listen to the cassette first.

17 Test yourself

Here are some areas from the Revision Unit in your Student's Book. How well do you think you can do them now? Put a tick (√) in the box.

Now do this test and see if you are right!

I can do it:	very well	OK	a little
1 Use new words.			
2 Use the past tense negative.			
3 Use past tense regular and irregular verbs.			
4 Ask questions about the past.			
5 Give reactions.			

1 Word groups

Vocabulary

Put the words in the columns.

cats cheese dogs leather ice meat cows milk oil sheep snow wool

Things that we get from animals	Types of animals	Things from nature

Put one of the words in the sentences.

1 Mr and Mrs Simon found the Iceman in the ....
2 The Iceman wore .... boots filled with grass.
3 He had clothes made from ...., so we know that he had sheep.
4 He had a bow and arrows, so he probably hunted animals and ate ....

2 Questions about the Iceman

Past tense negatives

Look at the pictures and answer Sarah's questions. Use these verbs.

have wear watch live go speak eat

SARAH: How did the Iceman tell the time?

YOU: *I don't know! He didn't have a watch!*

SARAH: What did the Iceman wear?

YOU: *I don't know! He didn't ...*

SARAH: What did the Iceman do in the evenings?

YOU: ....

SARAH: What did the Iceman live in?

YOU: ....

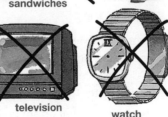
sandwiches

television

watch

trousers

English

house

SARAH: What language did the Iceman speak?

YOU: ....

SARAH: What did the Iceman eat?

YOU: ....

📼 You can check your answers on the cassette.

---

3 The Aztec ball game

Past simple: regular and irregular verbs

The Aztecs played a game like basketball. Read the rules of the game.

spectators

HOW TO PLAY THE BALL GAME
1 Two teams play with a ball.
2 The players try to put the ball through the hole.
3 The players cannot touch the ball with their hands, feet or head.
4 The game stops when the ball goes through the hole.
5 The winning team chases the spectators.
6 They catch the spectators.
7 They take the spectators' clothes.
8 They eat their food.

Now fill the gaps with the correct verbs in the the past tense.

use   try   touch   play   stop   put   eat   watch

The ball game

People from many countries in America played this game. The Aztecs ____(1)____ the game with two teams and a ball. Each team ____(2)____ to push the ball through the ring, similar to basketball. In the ball game, the Aztecs did not ____(3)____ the ball with their hands or feet. They only ____(4)____ their arms and legs. When one team ____(5)____ the ball through the hole, the game ____(6)____. The winning team didn't win a prize. They ____(7)____ to take the clothes of the people who ____(8)____ the game. They also ____(9)____ their food.

📼 You can check your answers on the cassette.

---

4 An Aztec quiz

Past tense questions

Read some more about the Aztecs.

LIFE WITH THE AZTECS

The Aztecs lived about 500 years ago in Mexico. They were very good farmers and fishermen. They ate a good diet of fish, meat and vegetables. The rich people wore cotton clothes and the poor people made clothes from plants.

The Aztecs had many gods, but their most important god was Huitzilopochtli. Huitzilopochtli was the sun god. The Aztecs believed that he worked all night to make the sun rise in the morning. Every morning, the Aztecs killed many prisoners in the market square to make their god happy.

Here are some answers about the Aztecs. What are the questions? For example:

1 When *did the Aztecs live*?

    500 years ago.

2 Where ....?

    In Mexico.

3 Who ....?

    Huitzilopochtli.

4 What ....?

    They killed many prisoners.

5 Why ....?

    To make their god happy.

6 What ....?

    They were farmers and fishermen.

7 What ....?

    They wore clothes from cotton.

---

5 What do you say?

Giving reactions

Read (and listen) to what Sarah says. What can you say in reply?

SARAH: I had a strange week last week. On Monday, I had a big History test.

YOU: ....

SARAH: I didn't pass!

YOU: ....

SARAH: On Tuesday I had a Maths test, and I got all the answers right!

YOU: ....

SARAH: And then, on Wednesday, I ate too much ice cream and I was ill.

YOU: ....

SARAH: On Thursday, I dropped my radio. It doesn't work now.

YOU: ....

SARAH: But on Friday, I found ten pounds in the road.

YOU: ....

SARAH: I'm going to buy a new radio now. Bye!

You can check your answers with the cassette.
Now look back at the chart at the beginning of this Unit. Were you right?

A picture dictionary (3)

Complete the timeline.

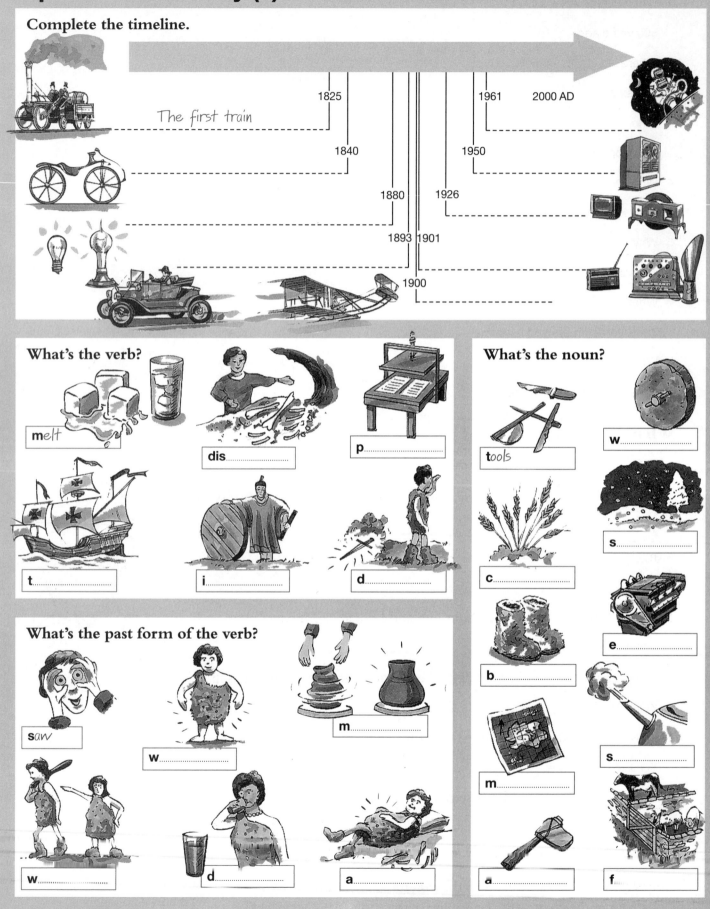

The first train

1825 1840 1880 1893 1901 1900 1926 1950 1961 2000 AD

What's the verb?

melt

dis...................

p...................

t...................

i...................

d...................

What's the past form of the verb?

saw

w...................

m...................

w...................

d...................

a...................

What's the noun?

tools

w...................

c...................

s...................

b...................

e...................

m...................

s...................

a...................

f...................

Topic 18 Climates of the world

---

1 World climates
Vocabulary

Read the definitions and choose the correct word.
(Look at pages 152–3 in your Student's Book.)

warm temperate tropical polar monsoon desert cool temperate tundra

1 In a .... climate, the winters are not normally very cold.

2 The rainforests are in areas with a .... climate.

3 During the day the temperature can rise to 52°C and at night it gets very cold in areas with a .... climate.

4 In a .... climate, it usually rains for five months of the year and is dry for seven months.

5 There aren't any trees in a region with a .... climate.

6 In a .... climate it rains nearly all the year round.

7 In the summer, the hottest temperature in a .... climate is less than 10°C.

---

2 The Beaufort scale
Reading

2.1 The wind

Every climate has wind. The Beaufort scale is a way of measuring the wind.

Match the descriptions (a–l) to the correct pictures.

a Trees fly through the air.
b A flag can fly.
c Small trees move.
d Leaves move.
e Smoke moves gently in the air.
f Parts of trees break off.

g Small branches move.
h It is very difficult to walk.
i Some things outside break.
j A hurricane!
k Large branches move.
l Damage to houses.

Force 1 5 kph | Force 2 10 kph | Force 3 15 kph | Force 4 20 kph | Force 5 30 kph | Force 6 40 kph

Force 7 50 kph | Force 8 65 kph | Force 9 75 kph | Force 10 90 kph | Force 11 105 kph | Force 12 120 kph

2.2 Why are there hurricanes?

Read about how a hurricane starts.
Draw a picture for each part. Label the pictures.

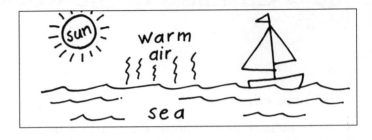

The sun warms the sea.

Water vapour rises into the air. Cold air comes down
and goes round and round in a spiral.
This is the 'eye' of the hurricane.

More and more water vapour goes up and more and
more cold air comes down. The cold air goes round
faster and faster. The wind blows at 125 kmph. The
'eye' of the hurricane is calm.

Hurricanes can move very fast. They are very
dangerous. They can pull up trees and destroy
houses and towns.

Compare your pictures with other students in your next lesson.

3   Say it clearly!

3.1 Same spelling – different sound!

/iː/: *eat*
/eə/: *wear*
/ɪə/: *year*
/e/: *weather*

 This letter pattern '–ea–' has four different sounds. Listen and repeat.

/iː/ eat   /eə/ wear   /ɪə/ year   /e/ weather

You can practise two sounds here.

3.2 The /iː/ sound: eat

 Listen and repeat.

meat   weak   repeat   heal   beach   please   meal   clean   leaf

I like going to the beach.   I clean my teeth after every meal.

Choose some words and make your own sentences. Record them if you can.

3.3 The /e/ sound: weather

🔊 Listen and repeat.

weather   leather   dead   healthy   head   feather

We get leather from cows.   I use an umbrella in wet weather.

Choose some words and make your own sentences. Record them if you can.

---

4   Meet Winnie!

Talking about the weather

Write your answers to Winnie's questions.

WINNIE: Hello! My name's Winnie. What's your name?

YOU: ....

WINNIE: I've got a letter from my grandmother. She lives in Jamaica. It's always hot there. Is it always hot in your country?

YOU: ....

WINNIE: Well, my grandmother says it's about 25 degrees in Jamaica. What's the temperature where you are now?

YOU: ....

WINNIE: The climate in Jamaica is tropical. It rains very heavily. Do you have heavy rain in your country?

YOU: ....

WINNIE: Oh. Sometimes, in Jamaica, they have terrible storms and hurricanes. What about you?

YOU: ....

WINNIE: Next year, I want to go and see my grandmother on holiday. Where do you go for your holidays?

YOU: ....

WINNIE: That's nice. I have to go now. I want to write a letter to my grandmother. Bye.

YOU: ....

🔊 You can talk to Winnie on the cassette.

---

5   Sing a song! Here comes the sun

🔊 See page 155 in your Student's Book for the words to 'Here comes the sun'.

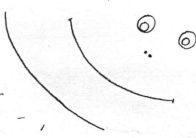

Language focus

1 What's going to happen?

'going to'

1.1 They're going to …

Write a sentence for each picture.

They're going to crash.

....

....

1.2 Which one is a plan?

Look at Exercise 1.1. Which pictures show something that is *a plan*?

Which pictures show something that is *certain to happen*?

Plans: *b,* .... Certain to happen: ....

Write some more examples of your own.

....

2 You have to …

'have to'

Tom made a cake in the kitchen, but look at the mess! What do you think his father is saying? Write five or six sentences about what the boy *has to* do.

3 Talk to Sarah

In a café

You're in a café with Sarah. Look at the menu and write your answers to Sarah's questions.

SARAH: Hello. Sorry I'm late! Are you hungry?

YOU: _____

SARAH: I am. Do you know what you are going to have first?

YOU: _____

SARAH: Well, I think I'm going to have melon first. What are you going to have after that?

YOU: _____

SARAH: Mmm. That sounds good. Oh, here's the waitress. Can you tell her what you are going to have?

WAITRESS: What would you like?

YOU: _____

SARAH: And can I have melon and then spaghetti, please?

WAITRESS: Sorry, there's no spaghetti.

SARAH: Oh dear. A cheese omelette then, please. What are you going to have afterwards?

YOU: _____

SARAH: That sounds good. I'm going to have that, too. Are you going to have cola or orange juice?

YOU: _____

SARAH: Can I have water, please? Thank you. Now, how are you?

You can talk to Sarah on the cassette.

MENU
Melon, soup, salad
Hamburger & chips, fish & rice, spaghetti carbonara, omlette.
Fruit, cake, apple pie.
Drinks: orange juice, milk, cola, mineral water, milk shake.

---

4 Say it clearly!

4.1 /h/

Many words in English begin with 'h'. Listen and repeat these words:

eat heat   at hat   it hit   and hand   eye high   old hold
art heart   ear hear

4.2 What do you hear?

Now listen again. Underline the word you hear and repeat it.

eat/heat   at/hat   it/hit   and/hand   eye/high   old/hold   art/heart   ear/hear

20 Fluency practice In the desert

1 What do you know?

What do you know about deserts?
Are these sentences true [T] or false [T]?

1 Nothing can live in a desert. ☐
2 The largest desert is in Africa. ☐
3 It is always hot in a desert. ☐

4 There isn't any water in a desert. ☐
5 The deserts we have today are not very old. ☐
6 The deserts are smaller today than 1,000 years ago. ☐

Look on page 57 to check your answers.

2 The deserts are getting bigger!

Deserts are bigger today than they were many years ago. Read and find out why.
The text gives three reasons. What are they?

Reason 1: ....

Reason 2: ....

Reason 3: ....

DESERTS ARE GROWING!

Today more than 20% of land is desert, but this is growing. This picture, for example, from a cave in Algeria, shows cows and people. The area was very green, and plants and grass grew there. Many types of animals lived there. The picture is more than three thousand years old. Today, the cave is in a desert. Why are the deserts growing? There are three main reasons.

One reason is climate. The climate changed and rain did not come every year. The sun is very hot and all the water in the land disappeared.

Another reason is animals. For hundreds of years, people near deserts had goats. Goats like eating plants. If they eat the plants, there aren't any plants to stop the wind. When the wind comes, it takes all the good soil. Soon, there isn't any good soil and it is very difficult for plants to grow.

A third reason is people. People cut down trees, and trees stop the wind. Also, in some countries, people wanted to make electricity. They changed the direction of the rivers and they built dams. This changed the direction of the water underground in other countries.

In places this is a very big problem. In the Sahel in Africa, thousands of people died between 1968 and 1974 because there was no water. We have to be very careful what we do with nature.

The Sahara Desert, Africa: the largest in the world. It is 7.7 million sq.km - bigger than Australia.

3 Choose the picture

Look at these pictures. They show the three reasons for deserts. Write a sentence about each picture.

Why are the deserts growing?

....

....

....

4 Imagine ...

Imagine that you are in a desert. What is it like there?
How do you feel? What can you see? What are you doing?
Write a paragraph about your ideas.

I'm in the desert. It is ...

....

....

....

....

Answers

1 False. There are many animals and plants that live in deserts. Most of the animals only come out at night, when it is not so hot. 2 True. The Sahara is the largest desert in the world. 3 False. At night it can be very cold in a desert. 4 False. There is often water underground. Sometimes the water comes out and makes an oasis. 5 False. They are over 3 million years old. 6 False. Some deserts are getting bigger. Read Exercise 2 and find out why!

Unit 20 Fluency practice **Theme D**   57

Help yourself with grammar

2 1

In Level 1, you saw two ways to help you learn grammar.
You can see them again in this Unit, and see one more way.

From Level 1

1 Cut and mix

1 Copy some sentences onto a piece of paper.

I had a test yesterday

I drank a lot of milk yesterday

Helen wore Ali's sweater

My brother made a cake last night

2 Cut each paper into three parts: subject, verb and object.

My brother | made | a cake last night

Helen | wore | Ali's sweater

3 Mix them up.

a test yesterday *I* *wore* *Ali's sweater* *had* *made* *My brother* *cake last night* *Helen* *I* *drank* *a lot of milk yester...*

4 Make some new sentences. (You can make some strange sentences!)

I | had | a lot of milk yesterday

My brother | wore | a cake last night

Look in your *Language Records* after the *Language focus* Units.
Find four more sentences. Cut them up and make some new sentences.

2 Write your own sentences

Take a sentence from your Student's Book:

The village people didn't use money …

Describe it: | Subject | + | didn't | + | verb | + | object |

Write five more sentences.

1 The village people didn't have telephones.

2 The village people ....

3 My friends didn't ....

4 ....

5 ....

Now you try it, with this sentence.

I'm going to meet my friend at 6 o'clock.

Describe it:

[ ] + [ ] + [ ] + [ ]

Write five more sentences.

....

....

....

....

Find another sentence. Describe it, and then write five more sentences.

Another way to help you learn vocabulary

3 Change some sentences

Look at how you can change a sentence.   They live in a city.
You can make it negative.   They don't live in a city.
You can make it into a question.   Do they live in a city?
You can put it in the past.   They lived in a city.
You can put it in the future.   They are going to live in a city.

Now you try it with this sentence. Make five changes.
(Check you know what it means!)

He works in a factory.

....

....

Find two more sentences from your Student's Book and make five changes to each one.

Sentence:

....

....

....

Sentence:

....

....

....

Use these three ways to practise the grammar in Units 22–27.

22 Revision The Tuareg people

---

1 A puzzle

Vocabulary

Read the clues. Write the word on the puzzle. The last letter of one word is the first letter of the next one.

1 A forest ...... can destroy hundreds of trees in a few hours.
2 This is the largest land animal.
3 The day after today.
4 England has a very ...... climate
5 There are a lot of ...... in a rainforest.
6 It did not rain here for six years.
7 Many parts of The Netherlands are below sea ....
8 In North Europe we wear ...... clothes in summer.
9 Mediterranean countries have a warm ...... climate.
10 'I haven't got ...... money to buy those shoes.'
11 A ...... is a strong wind which comes from the sea.
12 Cars are destroying the ....
13 Bananas grow in a ...... climate.

Now write the letters on the ⬚ squares here.

⬚ ⬚ ⬚ ⬚ ⬚ ⬚ ⬚ ⬚ ⬚

What word can you make with them? (Clue: in England it changes every day!)

T _ _ _ _ _ _ _ _ _ E

Write another puzzle like this for your friends to do.

---

2 What are they going to do?

'going to'

Look at the pictures. Write a sentence about each picture.

....

....

---

3 The Tuareg people

3.1 A true story: a problem for the Tuareg people

Read about the Tuareg people in the Sahara Desert.

The Sahara desert is one of the driest and hottest parts of the world. There, temperatures can rise to 55°C at mid-day. It is a very difficult place to live in, but it is home for the Tuareg people. They share the desert with wild animals such as elephants, snakes and lizards. The Tuaregs look after their goats.

For many years, the Tuaregs moved from place to place. In the past, the rain came every July and the Tuaregs, their goats, the elephants and other wild animals moved to the rivers and water holes. Every year, at the same time, the Tuaregs went to the markets to buy and sell camels and buy food for their journies. This was the way the Tuareg people lived.

But now the climate is changing and the Tuaregs have to change their way of life. The rain doesn't come every July. There isn't enough water in the desert for the goats and the wild animals. The Tuaregs cannot travel in the desert with their camels and goats. They have to stay in a village all the time. The children look after the goats in the villages and they go to school. The Tuaregs grow fruit and vegetables next to little rivers.

The changing climate changed the Tuaregs' way of life. Now it is changing the elephants' way of life! The desert is too dry for the elephants. They cannot find all the water they need (600 litres a day!) so they break the walls around the Tuareg's gardens and eat the bananas and pineapples that the Tuaregs grow. What can the Tuaregs do?

3.2 What can the Tuaregs do?

What can the Tuaregs do about the elephants? Write down some ideas.

I think they can ....

....

....

3.3 What do the Tuaregs have to do now?

The climate changed the life of the Tuaregs.
What do they *have to* do now?
What don't they *have to* do?
Write some sentences about these things:

- look after their gardens
- move from place to place
- look for the water holes
- build stronger garden walls
- travel to the markets

....

....

....

....

A picture dictionary (4)

Label the pictures.

d.....................

c.....................

hurricane

s.....................

r.....................

f.....................

f.....................

w.....................

i.....................

s.....................

What's the verb?

reflect

b.....................

p.....................

d**es**.....................

p.....................

r.....................

c..................... d.....................

What's the noun?

mountain

v.....................

b.....................

c.....................

r..................... h.....................

What's the adjective?

flat

w.....................

h.....................

d.....................

s..................... l..................... w.....................

23 Topic **The global village**

1 What's the word?

Vocabulary

1.1 The odd one out

Look at these words. Which word in each group is different from the other words?
Give a reason. For example:

1 sugar   bananas   (radio)   tea   coffee

   Radio is different. All the other things are primary products.

2 newspaper   magazine   book   (tree)   comic

   Tree. All the other things are made from ....

3 computers   cars   wheat   televisions   compact discs

   ....

4 jeans   T-shirt   bag   socks   dress

   ....

5 potatoes   rice   cheese   wheat   tomatoes

   ....

6 guitar   radio   Walkman   CD player   record player

   ....

7 sandwich   lemonade   milk   water   cola

   ....

8 car   bus   bicycle   lorry   train

   ....

9 iron   gold   copper   tin   sugar

   ....

10 football   cricket   tennis   swimming   handball

   ....

11 office   factory   park   shop   school

   ....

1.2 A puzzle

Write your answers from Exercise 1.1 in the correct space in the puzzle.
What do they spell?

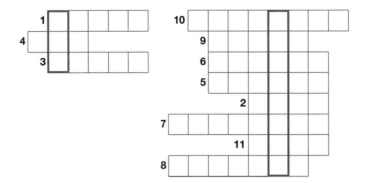

2   What are they made from?

Writing

How many primary products can you find in Exercise 1?
Choose four, and make a list of the things we can make from each one.

Gold is a primary product. We make coins, jewellery, and watches from gold.

....

....

....

....

3   Say it clearly!

/ə/: *copper, leather,*
rubber; /ʃ/ *sh*

3.1 /ə/

This is a very common sound in English. We use it when the sound is unstressed.
▭ Listen to the words with /ə/. Underline the strongest syllable.

paper   leather   copper   rubber   number   computer   sugar

▭ Listen again and repeat the words.

3.2 Say the sentences

▭ Listen and repeat the sentences.

My lucky number is three.   My shoes are made of leather.
I like sugar in my tea.   I like writing on the computer.

3.3 /ʃ/ sh

▭ The '-tio-' spelling often sounds like 'sh'. Listen and repeat.

education   dictionary   action   communication   station   connection

3.4 Say the sentences

Listen and repeat the sentences.

Where is the station?   Do you like action films?   Can I have a dictionary?

4   Talk to Sarah

Talk to Sarah about shops and shopping.

SARAH: Hello. How are you?

YOU: ....

SARAH: I'm fine. I went shopping this morning with my friends. I bought
         lots of things. Do you go shopping with your friends?

YOU: ....

SARAH: Well, first I went to the music shop and I bought a CD. Do you like
         music?

YOU: ....

SARAH: Then we went to a computer shop. My friend wanted to look at the
         games. Have you got any computer games?

YOU: ....

SARAH: After that, we went to market. They sell T-shirts there. Have you got
         a market in your town?

YOU: ....

SARAH: I bought a T-shirt there, and then I bought some sweets and some
         magazines. What type of magazines do you like?

YOU: ....

SARAH: Well, after that, I didn't have enough money for the bus. I had to
         walk home! Next month I'm going to save my money. Do you save
         any money?

YOU: ....

SARAH: Well, I have to go now. Talk to you soon. Bye.

You can talk to Sarah on the cassette.

5   Sing a song! Big money

See page 156 in your Student's Book for
the words to 'Big money'.

24 Language focus

1 Could you ...?

Requests with 'could'

Look at these pictures. What do you think each person is saying?
Write your answers.

Yes, of course.

TOWN 12 Km

No problem: I'm going that way.

Of course. Where are you going?

Yes, it's easy!

📼 You can check your answers on the cassette.

2 Would you like ... ?

Offers with 'would'

2.1 What's the answer?

Choose the correct reply (a–f).

1 Would you like a cold drink?
2 Would you like to go to the cinema on Friday?
3 Would you like a hamburger?
4 Would you like to go to the school disco?
5 Would you like that cassette for your birthday?
6 Would you like help with your homework?

a No thanks, I don't like that kind of music.
b No thanks, I don't eat meat.
c Yes please, I feel very thirsty.
d Yes please! I think she's a great singer!
e No thanks, I don't like cinemas.
f Yes please, I can't understand it at all.

📼 You can check your answers on the cassette.

2.2 What's the question?

Look at the pictures. Write what you can say.

Would you like ...

1 ....

2 ....

3 ....

Would you like to ...

1 ....

2 ....

3 ....

---

3 Enough is enough

'enough'

3.1 What are they saying?

Can you complete the speech bubbles? Use 'enough'.
Remember: *enough* comes *before* a noun but *after* an adjective.

a
They aren't ....
....

b
I'm not ....
....

c
Have you got ....
...........................?

e
I haven't got ....
....

d
Is that ....
...........................?

f
The ladder isn't ....
....

3.2 A poem

Read the poem.

When is enough enough?

Enough is too much
When it's a horrible dinner
At grandma's and she says:
'Have some more dear.
That's not enough food
For a big child like you.'
And I say: 'Thanks, Gran.
I've had enough, really.'

Enough is too little
When it's delicious ice cream
Of mum's and she says:
'That's enough now, dear.
That's enough for one day.
Save some for later.'

And I say 'Oh, Mum.
That's not enough!
Can I have just a bit more?'
And she says: 'Enough is enough'.

Can you tell me, please?
When is enough enough?

---

4 Say it clearly!

/ʌ/ cut

Notice the two different sounds.

4.1 /ʌ/ cut

🔈 Listen and say the words.

bus   summer   up   cut   enough   jump   under   suddenly

He jumped up suddenly.   There aren't enough buses in this town .

cut

4.2 /ʊ/ put

🔲 Listen and say the words.

put sugar pull could cook look book would

Would you like to look at my book?

Could you put sugar in my drink please?

---

5 Around town

Asking the way (1)

5.1 What's the name?

Look at the map. Can you write the name of each place (a–i) on a separate piece of paper?

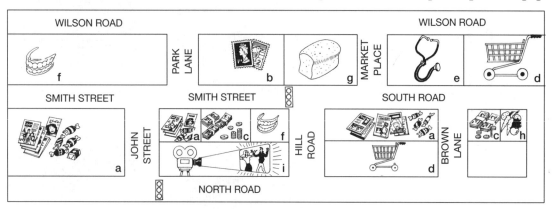

5.2 Where is it?

Now write your answers to these questions. Use:

between … and …   in front of   behind   on the left of …   on the right of …   next to

PERSON 1: Excuse me. Can you tell me if there is a bank near here?

YOU: Yes, of course. There's one in Smith Street, between the newsagent's and the dentist's.

PERSON 2: Hello. Do you know if there's a supermarket near here?

YOU: ....

PERSON 3: Excuse me. Can you tell me where the cinema is?

YOU: ....

PERSON 4: Hello. Do you know if there's a doctor's near here?

YOU: ....

PERSON 5: Excuse me. Can you tell me where the post office is?

YOU: ....

PERSON 6: Excuse me. Can you tell me if there's a dentist's near here?

YOU: ....

🔲 You can talk to each person on the cassette.

Fluency practice   Three regions in Britain

1   Mountains, farms and factories

Reading

Read the descriptions of three regions in Britain and answer these questions.

Which regions have a lot of sheep farms? ....

Which region has a lot of big cities in it? ....

Which region has a lot of jobs, do you think? ....

Which region would *you* like to live in? ....

The Highlands
Glasgow
Edinburgh
Snowdonia
Birmingham
The Midlands
Cardiff
London

The Highlands

THE HIGHLANDS, *in Scotland*

In the winter, many people come to this region to go skiing. Many people who live here are sheep farmers. They live in 'crofts' (a Scottish word for a small farm). There aren't many villages or towns in this region. Young people often leave the region when they are 18. They go to study and work in the big cities like Glasgow and Edinburgh.

THE MIDLANDS, *in England*

This region is a long way from the sea. Two hundred years ago, they built canals to take raw materials to the factories and to take the manufactured goods to the other cities and to the ports. Many people here work in the car, steel and clothes factories. In their free time, people like to walk near the canals and go fishing.

Snowdonia

The Midlands

SNOWDONIA, *in Wales*

Snowdonia is a beautiful region in North West Wales. Many people come here to climb the mountains and walk through the quiet villages and woods.

There are a lot of sheep farmers in the region. They do not grow many crops because the soil is not very good.

It is also very windy and cold in the winter. In the past, people worked in the gold and copper mines, but they are closed now. Many people here are bilingual. They speak Welsh at home and at school, but they can also speak English.

2 In your region

Think about where you live. Make some notes about these questions.

What does your area look like? Is it very flat? Are there many trees and mountains?
Is it near the sea?

....

Are there many factories and offices in your area? What do they make?

....

Do young people stay in the area where you live?

....

Where do people go in the evenings and at weekends?

....

Now use your notes to write about your area on a separate piece of paper.

My area is ...
There are ...
People work ...
When young people leave school, they usually ...
In their free time, people like to ...

3 Talk to Sarah about your region

Write your answers to Sarah's questions.

SARAH: Hello. Tell me about where you live.

YOU: ....

SARAH: Ah! That sounds interesting. Do you like it?

YOU: ....

SARAH: What do you do in your free time in the evenings?

YOU: ....

SARAH: And what do you do at the weekends?

YOU: ....

SARAH: I've got a job at the weekend. Is it easy to get a job where you live?

YOU: ....

SARAH: I'm going to my weekend job now. I'll talk to you again later. Bye.

YOU: ....

📠 You can talk to Sarah on the cassette.

26 Help yourself with a dictionary

A bilingual dictionary can tell you a lot of things.
In this Unit, you can see some ways that a dictionary can help you.

1 What's in your dictionary?

Your dictionary can give you a lot of information.
Look at your dictionary. Does it have any of these things? Tick (√) the box.

List of irregular verbs ☐
Useful phrases ☐
Pronunciation guide ☐
List of abbreviations ☐
Grammar section ☐
Weights and measures ☐
Other things ☐

Weights and measures

Weights
1 kg = 0.45359 lbs

Pronunciation guide

Long vowels
/iː/ feed, /uː/ food

Grammar section

Articles
The indefinite article
'a' or 'an' is used to
refer to

Irregular verbs

Infinitive	Past simple	Past participle
be	was/were	been

Useful phrases

Shopping
I'm looking for a

Asking for directions
Can you tell me how to find

List of abbreviations

AA   Automobile Association

2 Information about a word

2.1 What can it tell you?

A good dictionary can give you a lot of information about a word.

It can tell you how to say the word.

It can tell you what type of word it is.

If it is an irregular verb, it can give you the past tense.

It can give you the meaning.

It can give you the correct spelling.

see [siː] *v, pt* saw, *pp* seen (a) (general) *ver*; I can't see her. *No la veo.*, I saw them at the party. *Los ví en la fiesta.*; (b) (understand) *entender, comprender*; I see! *¡Ya entiendo!*

It can give you some examples.

2.2 What type of word is it?

Look in your dictionary. What *type* of word is each one of these words?

noun   verb   adjective   preposition   adverb

bread ....   in ....   speak ....

make ....   out ....   quickly ....

2.3 **Find the past form**

Look in your dictionary and find the past form of these verbs.

get ....   sing ....   wake ....

drink ....   hit ....

2.4 **How do you say it?**

Check the pronunciation of these English words. Notice how the same letters have different sounds.

enough   through   year   teacher   cat   centre

---

3   What does it mean?

3.1 Which meaning do you need?

Many words have different meanings. Sometimes the meaning of the verb is different from the noun. Find these words in your dictionary. Write the meaning in your language.

spring (verb)   spring (noun)   flat (adjective)   flat (noun)
light (verb)   light (noun)   light (adjective)   fish (noun)   fish (verb)
well (adjective)   well (adverb)   well (noun)

3.2 Check it!

If you find a word that you need, check it! Look in the other half of the dictionary to check the meaning.

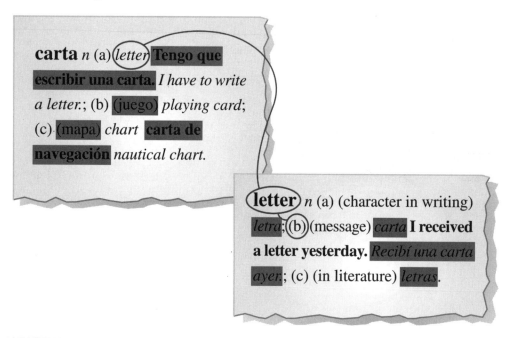

Read these sentences. Find the underlined word in your dictionary and the correct translation. Find the same meaning in the other half of your dictionary.

He lives in a <u>flat</u>.   We get water from a <u>well</u>.   In <u>spring</u>, the flowers start to appear.

27 Test yourself

Here are some things you learned to do in Units 23–26. How well can you do them? Put a tick (√) in the box.

I can do it:	very well	OK	a little
1 Ask someone to do something.			
2 Offer someone something.			
3 Use 'enough'.			
4 Use the new words.			
5 Ask the way.			

1 What do you say?

Asking someone to do something

What do you say in these situations? Use 'could …'

1 Your watch is broken. You want to know the time.

Could you ....?

2 You can't understand your homework. Ask a friend. ....?

3 You don't understand an English word. Your friend has a dictionary. ....?

4 Your friend has got a new video. You want to watch it. ....?

5 You haven't got any money with you, and you want to buy some sweets. What do you say to your friend?

....?

2 Offering someone something

Offering someone something: 'would'

Look at the pictures. What are the people saying?

Would you …?

3 Where does 'enough' go?

'enough'

Where can you put 'enough' in these sentences – at a↓, b↓ or c↓?
Write the complete sentence.

a↓   b↓   c↓
1 He's not old to drive a car.

....

a↓   b↓   c↓
2 I haven't got money to go to the concert.

....

a↓   b↓   c↓
3 She didn't run fast to win the race .

....

a↓   b↓ c↓
4 The water isn't hot for a bath.

....

a↓   b↓ c↓
5 My mother says I don't eat fruit.

....

4 New words

Vocabulary

Read the clues and fill in the words. What is the word going down?

1 Buy things from another country: i..............

2 My radio was m.............. in Japan.

3 A very important metal: i..............

4 Car tyres are made from r..............

5 It comes from wheat. We use it to make bread.

   f..............

6 Money that you get when you work: w..............

7 My shirt is made of c..............

8 Sell to another country: e..............

9 Some people put s.............. in their tea and coffee.

10 In a television, there are a lot of w..............

11 A person from another country: f..............

5 Find out where Winnie lives!

5.1 Talk to Winnie

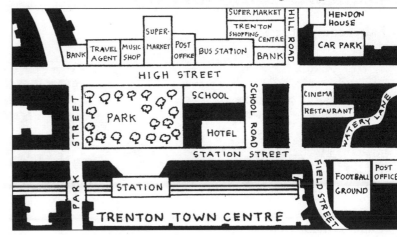

📼 Look at the map. Talk to Winnie.

Mark her house on the map.

WINNIE: Hello! How are you?

YOU: ....

WINNIE: I don't know your address. Could you tell me what it is?

YOU: ....

WINNIE: Thanks. I'm going to write it in my book. Have you got my address?

YOU: ....

WINNIE: Would you like to come to my house next weekend?

YOU: ....

WINNIE: Great! Look at the map of Trenton. I can show you where I live.

YOU: ....

WINNIE: Can you find the station opposite the park in Station Street?

YOU: ....

WINNIE: On the other side of the park is the High Street. Can you see a bank next to the bus station?

YOU: ....

WINNIE: Near there is Hill Road. There's a big supermarket there. Opposite the supermarket there is a block of flats. It's called 'Hendon House' and I live there. Flat number 26. What time can you come on Saturday?

YOU: ....

WINNIE: Great! See you then. Bye!

📼 Listen to Winnie on the cassette.

5.2 Winnie's address

Write Winnie's address in the address book.

A picture dictionary (5)

Label the pictures.

Paper is made from *wood*

Books are ....

Cars ....

Bread ....

Clothes ....

Sweets ....

What's the noun?

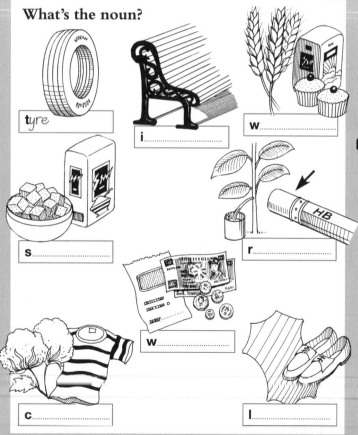

t*yre*

i...

w...

s...

r...

w...

c...

l...

What's the adjective?

d*irty*

fl...

e...

d...

d...

n...

Topic Blackout!

1 What's the word?

Vocabulary

Write the correct word into the squares. What do they spell?

1 A machine that makes electricity. (g......)

2 When the blackout happened in New York, some people were trapped inside a l..... .

3 A positive electron and another positive electron r...... each other.

4 A machine that makes electricity from water power is a hydro-e...... generator.

5 Problems. (t......)

6 Past of break. (b......)

7 In New York, during the blackout, only the car l...... were working.

8 A country next to the United States of America. (C......)

9 + = positive, - = n...... .

10 Positive electrons a...... negative electrons.

11 All the people. (e......)

2 Talk to a news reporter

Writing and speaking

Imagine that *you* were in the New York blackout. Where were you? Were you in danger? What were you doing? What happened to you? Write your answers to the reporter's questions.

REPORTER: Excuse me, can I ask you some questions? Where were you when the lights went out?

YOU: ....

REPORTER: What were you doing?

YOU: ....

REPORTER: Was anybody with you?

YOU: ....

REPORTER: Were you frightened?

YOU: ....

REPORTER: Well, I would be frightened. What did you do?

YOU: ....

REPORTER: Yes, I think that was the right thing to do. What happened next?

YOU: ....

REPORTER: Just one last question, because I know you are very tired. What are you going to do now?

YOU: ....

REPORTER: Well, thank you very much for talking to me. You can see the news on television at 9 o'clock. If you've got any electricity! Goodbye.

YOU: ....

Now talk to the reporter on the cassette.

---

3 In the newspaper

Writing

Now you are a news reporter! Write a news story about what happened to you in the New York Blackout.

New York Times   *10 November 1965*

English Student in New York Blackout

Last night, an English student was ....

....

....

....

....

---

4 Say it clearly!

/s/

Open your mouth just a little and say /s/. Notice that there isn't a vowel before the 's'.

Listen and say the words and sentences.

space Spanish speak sit summer sun sky spring satellite

I like sitting in the sun in summer.
At night, I like looking at the sky.
There are lots of satellites in space.

ⱥspace

---

5 Sing a song I didn't do it (but all the lights went out)

A song

See page 156 in your Student's Book for the words to 'I didn't do it (but all the lights went out)'.

29 Language focus

1 A circular story

Past continuous

Can you put in the correct verbs in the spaces?
Use the Past continuous. (You can use each verb twice.)

sit
blow
cry
look
think
clean
sleep
sing
lean

You can check your answers with the cassette.

The Bandit's Story

The night was cold and dark. The bandits .... around the fire. They .... into the flames and they .... about the next day. The wind .... gently. Somewhere in the distance, a wolf .... One bandit .... softly. Another bandit .... his gun. Suddenly, the leader of the bandits shouted: 'Pancho! Tell us a story.'

Pancho ...., but he woke up. He .... against a tree. He stood up and walked to the fire. He sat down next to where the leader .... Everyone looked at him. He looked into their eyes and he told the following story.

'The night was cold and dark. The bandits .... around the fire. They .... into the flames and they .... about the next day. The wind .... gently. Somewhere in the distance, a wolf .... One bandit .... softly. Another bandit .... his gun. Suddenly, the leader of the bandits shouted: 'Pancho! Tell us a story.'

Pancho .... but he woke up. He .... against a tree. He stood up and walked to the fire. He sat down next to where the leader .... Everyone looked at him. He looked into their eyes and he told the following story …

2 What was happening?

Past continuous

Write a sentence for each picture. Say what *was happening* when something *happened*.
For example: She was eating a cake …   … when she found an insect.

3 Please don't touch!

Look at these pictures. What do you think the notice says in each situation?
Use your imagination!

4 Around town

Here's the map from Unit 24. Write your answers to the questions.
Tell each person where to go.

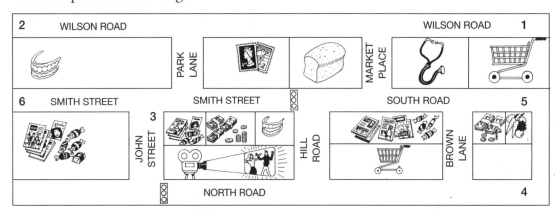

For example:

You are at place 1

> PERSON A: Excuse me, can you tell me how to get to Smith Street?
>
> YOU: Yes, of course. You go straight down Wilson Road. Take the first turning on the left and then turn right. Go straight on past the traffic lights. That's Smith Street.
>
> PERSON A: Thanks very much.
>
> YOU: Not at all.

You are at place 2

> PERSON B: Hello. Do you know how I can get to the cinema from here?
>
> YOU: ....
>
> ....
>
> PERSON B: Thank you.

You are at place 3

> PERSON C: Excuse me. Could you tell me the way to the supermarket in South Road?
>
> YOU: ....
>
> ....
>
> PERSON C: Thank you.

You are at place 4

> PERSON D: Hello. Do you know the way to the post office, please?
>
> YOU: ....
>
> ....
>
> PERSON D: Thanks a lot.

You are at place 5

> PERSON E: Excuse me. Could you tell me the way to the nearest baker's?
>
> YOU: ....
>
> ....
>
> PERSON E: Thank you very much.

You are at place 6

> PERSON F: Hello. Could you tell me the way to the nearest grocer's?
>
> YOU: ....
>
> ....
>
> PERSON F: Thanks.

---

5 Say it clearly!

/tʃ/ *cheese*

5.1 Say 'cheese'!

📼 Listen and say these words and sentences. Can you hear a 't' sound at the beginning of the 'ch' words?

cheese chop cheap chicken children church change chance check
beach branch watch touch teacher

Say cheese!
There are lots of children in the church.
Do chickens like cheese?

5.2 Don't say 't'

📼 Not all 'ch' words have the same pronunciation. Listen and say these words.

chemist character Christmas machine school

Fluency practice Invent something!

1 How to put sugar in your drink

Look at this invention. How does it work?
Write a paragraph to explain what happens.

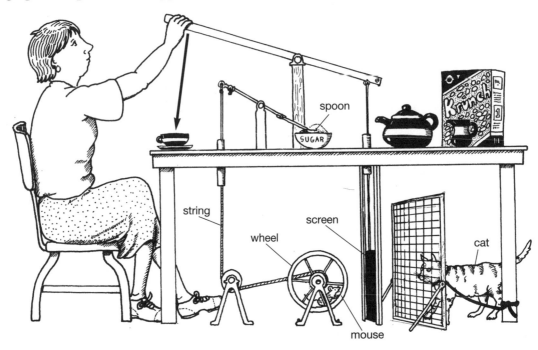

2 Invent something!

Choose one of these things (or make your own invention).
Draw a complete picture in the box to show how it works.

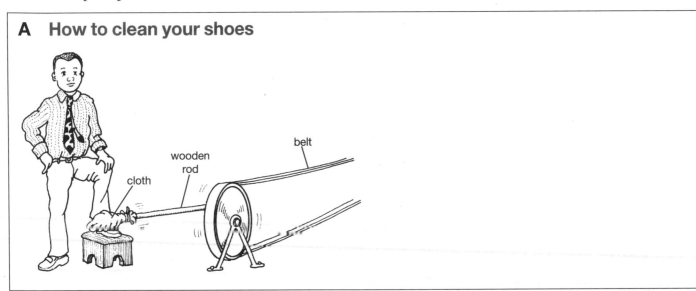

A How to clean your shoes

B How to answer the telephone

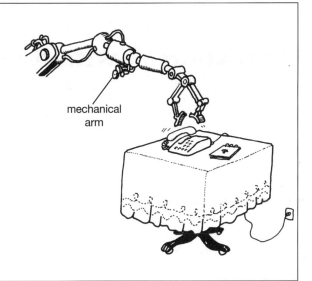

mechanical
arm

C How to wash the dishes

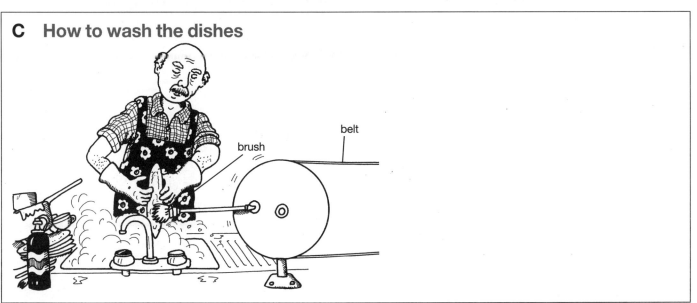

brush

belt

Explain what happens.

....

....

....

....

....

....

....

....

....

31 Help yourself with fluency

In Level 1, you saw three ways to help you with your fluency in English. You can see them again in this Unit, and see two more ways. Use them to practise your English after your lessons.
For this Unit you need some card, a tape recorder and an empty cassette.

From Level 1

1 Phrases in the bag

If you put some phrases on cards,
you can test yourself.

Useful phrases

> Can you tell me the way
> to the post office?

Write these phrases on some cards. Write them
in your language on the other side.

What do you think?	Reacting	In the classroom
What do you think of ...?	Brilliant!	Can you check this, please?
I think it's exciting.	How awful!	How do you spell '...'?
I don't mind it.	You lucky thing!	What does '...' mean?
I think it's a bit boring.	Oh, bad luck!	Can I have a dictionary, please?
I don't like it.		
It's awful.		

Find some more phrases in the Student's Book and make cards for them.
Put all the cards in a bag. Take out a card and say it in English or your language.

2 Talk to yourself

You can use a cassette player to
talk to yourself.

*Asking and
answering questions*

> Hello, what are you
> going to do next?

> Hello, what are you
> going to do next?

> I'm going to have
> my dinner.

Record these questions onto your cassette. (Wait a few seconds after each question.)

- Hello. How are you today?
- What did you do this morning?
- Did you do the same yesterday?
- What were you doing at this time yesterday?

- What are you going to do next?
- Can you tell the way to the nearest supermarket?
- Thanks! Bye!

Now talk to yourself. Play the cassette and answer your questions.
Find some more questions in your Student's Book and record them.

3 Have a conversation

You can imagine that you are two different people.

Choose one of the situations below and talk to yourself. Change your hat/chair/coat as you talk.

Good morning. How are you today?

Fine thanks, how are you?

The climate in your country
YOU 1: What's the climate like in your country?
YOU 2: Well, it's .... What's it like in your country?
YOU 1: ....

The food you eat
YOU 1: Hi. What's your favourite food?
YOU 2: ....
YOU 1: How many meals ....?
YOU 2: ....

The sports you play
YOU 1: Do you play any sports?
YOU 2: .... What about you?
YOU 1: ....

Choose some more topics to talk to yourself about.

Two new ways to help you with your fluency

4 Sing a song!

Choose a simple song (in your language or in English). Make up some new words. You can sing instead of talking!

Oh, hello. How are you today?

I'm fine. Where are you going?

I'm going to the cinema with a friend …

5 Practise with a friend

You can practise some situations with a friend. Choose a situation and take turns.

Excuse me, can you tell me the way to the nearest doctor's?

Talking about what you did

Last night, I …

You lucky thing!

Oh, how awful!

Saying what you think

What do you think about …?

I think it's …

Asking the way

Hello. Do you know the way to the post office, please?

Revision Puzzle page – in the town

PUZZLE BOX

1 How many things can you find that use electricity? Make a list.

lights in the street

2 There are five things wrong in the picture. Write a sentence about each one.

3 Where are these people?
What are they doing?

....

....

....

....

4 Find these people.
What were they doing 15 minutes ago?
Write a sentence about each one.

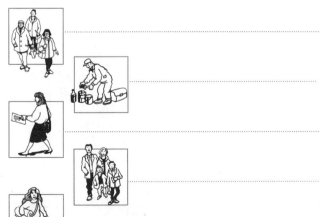

....

....

....

....

....

A picture dictionary (6)

Label the picture.

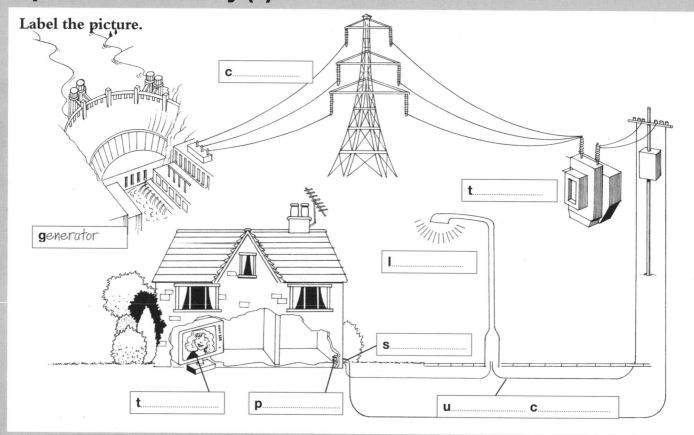

c...........................

t...........................

generator

l...........................

s...........................

t...........................

p...........................

u........................... c...........................

What's the noun?

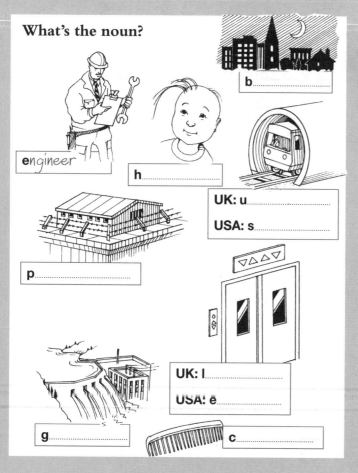

b...........................

engineer

h...........................

UK: u...........................

USA: s...........................

p...........................

UK: l...........................

USA: e...........................

g...........................

c...........................

What's the verb?

repair

t...........................

b................... d...........................

l...........................

f...........................

b...........................

r...........................

j........................... b........................... a...........................

Language summaries

Units 1 and 2

PRESENT SIMPLE: POSITIVE

You can use the Present simple to talk about:

– a fact or something that happens generally:

> I live in a castle.
> They drive a large car.

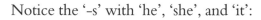

– something that happens regularly:

> I get up at 7 a.m.

Notice the '–s' with 'he', 'she', and 'it':

> She works in a office.
> He eats an apple every day.

PRESENT SIMPLE: NEGATIVES AND QUESTIONS WITH 'BE', 'HAVE GOT' AND 'CAN'

In sentences with 'be', 'have got' and 'can', you can add '–n't' or 'not' to make the negative:

> London isn't (is not) the capital of Italy.
> I haven't (have not) got a dog.
> She can't (cannot) ride a bicycle.

Questions are easy! Put the verb before the subject. Like this:

> Are they English?
> Can she swim?
> Has he got a dog?

PRESENT SIMPLE: ALL OTHER VERBS

To make the negative with other verbs, you add 'doesn't' ('does not') or 'don't' ('do not'):

> She doesn't (does not) live in Brazil. She lives in America.
> They don't (do not) play football at school. They play handball.
> We don't (do not) swim in the winter. It's too cold.

To make questions, you use 'do' or 'does':

> Does he speak English?
> Do they live near here?

Notice that you use 'does' for 'he/she/it':

> She doesn't know Peter.
> It doesn't work!

You can also put a question word at the beginning, like this:

> **When** do insects sleep?
> **Why** does an elephant live so long?
> **What** do spiders eat?
> **Where** do snakes sleep?
> **How long** does a horse live?
> **How** do birds fly?

ADJECTIVES

An adjective describes a noun. It goes *before* the noun. It does not change for singular or plural, masculine or feminine:

> Australia is a **big** country.
> David is a **happy** baby.
> They are **good** students.

POSSESSIVE ADJECTIVES: 'MY, YOUR, HIS HER' …

Possessive adjectives are words that say who something belongs to. They come *before* the noun:

> This is **my** dog.
>
> **His** horse is very old.

There is a different possessive adjective for each person, except 'you' (singular) and 'you' (plural):

Subject	Possessive adjective	Example
I	**my**	Where is my dog?
you (*sing.*)	**your**	What's your name?
he	**his**	That's his house.
she	**her**	Her horse is very old.
it	**its**	The cat sleeps in its basket.
we	**our**	This is our pet crocodile.
you (*pl.*)	**your**	Where is your mother?
they	**their**	Cows give milk to their babies.

You can also make possessives with names of people or things:

> This is Pat**'s** house.
>
> That's the dog**'s** food.

PERSONAL SUBJECT PRONOUNS: 'I, YOU, HE, SHE' …

Personal pronouns are subjects of the sentence. They come *before* the verb in positive sentences:

I am tired.

You are tall.

He is a student.

She is a doctor.

It is an elephant.

We are at school.

You are in the library.

They are French.

OBJECT PRONOUNS: 'ME, YOU, HIM, HER' …

Object pronouns are words for the object of an action. They come *after* the verb:

Subject	+ Verb	+ Object pronoun
This is my bedroom. I	like	it.

Subject	Object pronoun	Example
I	**me**	Can you help me?
you (*sing.*)	**you**	I can see you!
he	**him**	Do you know him?
she	**her**	I can telephone her.
it	**it**	Do you like it?
we	**us**	Good food is important for us.
you (*pl.*)	**you**	Where is your mother?
they	**them**	Vitamins are important. You need them!

COMPARATIVES AND SUPERLATIVES: WORDS WITH ONE SYLLABLE

You can compare things by putting '-er' and '-est' at the end of adjectives that have one syllable. For example:

> long tall big near fast old hot small
>
> Mercury is hot**ter** than the Earth.
> The Sun is the hot**test** thing in the solar system.
> Pluto is small**er** than Mercury.
> It is **the** small**est** planet in the solar system.

Notice small ➡ small**er** ➡ **the** small**est**

BUT hot ➡ hot**ter** ➡ the hot**test**.

Notice some exceptions:

good ➡ better ➡ the best

bad ➡ worse ➡ the worst

> Maths is good for us. History is better for you. English is the best for you!
> A dog bite is bad for you. A snake bite is worse for you. A shark bite is the worst for you!

COMPARATIVES AND SUPERLATIVES: WORDS WITH TWO OR MORE SYLLABLES

You use 'more …' and 'the most' to compare adjectives with more than one syllable:

This car is **more** expensive **than** that car.

This car is **the most** expensive.

I think swimming is **more** exciting **than** walking.

Windsurfing is **the most** exciting sport for me!

Adjectives that end with '-y' change to '-i-':

It is very windy today. It's much windier than yesterday.

He looks happy. He's the happiest man I know!

PRESENT CONTINUOUS

You can use the Present continuous to talk about something which is happening now.

Notice the form:

Positive:

Subject	+ 'be'	+ Verb + '-ing'	+ Object
He	is	coming down	the ladder.
They	are	flying into	space.

Questions:

'be'	+ Subject	+ Verb + '-ing'	+ Object
Is	he	driving	the moon car?
Is	he	opening	the door?

Negatives:

Subject	+ 'be' + 'not'	+ Verb + '-ing'	+ Object
The sun	isn't	shining	today.
We	aren't	working	today.

You can also use the Present continuous to talk about plans and definite events:

She's leaving school next year.

I'm singing in the concert tomorrow.

Past simple – see Themes B and C.

Theme A

SPECIAL VERBS: VERBS + '-ING'

Some verbs in English are 'special'. The verb *after* them usually has '-ing' at the end. Most or these verbs are about likes and dislikes:

like   hate   love   don't mind   dislike   enjoy

I **like** cook**ing**

I **love** rid**ing** my bicycle

or about starting and stopping:

start   stop   continue   finish   begin

I **started** learn**ing** English one year ago.

Can you **stop** talk**ing**, please?

ADVERBS

Adverbs *describe* the verb. They say *how* somebody or something did something. They usually come *after* the verb. For most adverbs, you add '-ly' to the adjective:

quick ➡ quick**ly** The dog eats his dinner quickly.

slow ➡ slow**ly** Please drive slowly near the school.

If the adjective has 'y' at the end, the adverb ends with '-ily':

happy ➡ happ**ily** The children played happily in the garden.

easy ➡ eas**ily** I did that homework easily.

Some adverbs are different!

good ➡ well   fast ➡ fast   hard ➡ hard

She speaks Spanish very well.

The cheetah can run very fast.

Before the race, the sportswoman trained very hard.

Theme B

PAST SIMPLE

You use the Past simple to talk about something at a certain time in the past. For example, 'yesterday', 'last night', 'in 1993' and '4,000 years ago'.

PAST SIMPLE: 'BE'

The past of 'be' is 'was' and 'were':

I	**was**	I was tired after the football match.
you (*sing.*)	**were**	You were late for school this morning.
he	**was**	He was President for five years.
she	**was**	She was a beautiful baby.
it	**was**	It was very cold last night.
we	**were**	We were in the cinema for three hours.
you (*pl.*)	**were**	You were all in the same group last year.
they	**were**	They were the best students in the class.

PAST SIMPLE: REGULAR VERBS

Some verbs are 'regular'. They all have '-ed' on the end. The '-ed' is the same for all the personal pronouns:

> I played table tennis yesterday.
> We walked home from school last Monday.
> They started their homework at six o'clock.

Theme C

PAST SIMPLE: IRREGULAR VERBS

Some verbs do not use '-ed'. They make the past form in different ways. Look at the list on page 149 in the Student's Book. The form is the same for all the pronouns:

> go ➡ went We went on holiday to France last year.
> make ➡ made My brother made a cake last week.
> see ➡ saw I saw Peter last Thursday.
> have ➡ had They had a lot of homework last night.

PAST SIMPLE: QUESTIONS AND NEGATIVES

Regular and irregular verbs use 'did' to make questions and negatives. Notice the form:

'Did'	+ Subject	+ Infinitive
Did	they	have computers 4,000 years ago?
Did	you	read the newspaper yesterday?

Subject	+ 'didn't'	+ Infinitive	+ Object
I	didn't	go	on holiday last year.
She	didn't	do	her homework last night.

You can also put a question word at the beginning:

> **When** did they invent the wheel?
> **Why** did the Iceman put grass in his boots?
> **How** did people in the past communicate?
> **How long** did people live 4,000 years ago?
> **What** did they do in the evenings?
> **Where** did they find the Iceman's body?

You can give a short answer:

> Did they live in houses? Yes, they did. *or*
>   No, they didn't.
> Did they travel to other villages? Yes, they did. *or*
>   No, they didn't.

Theme D

'GOING TO'

You can use 'going to' to talk about plans for the future:

> I am going to watch a film on television at 8 p.m.
> They're going to play ice hockey on Sunday.

You can also use 'going to' to talk about things that are certain to happen:

> Look at the sky. It's going to rain!
> He's not looking. He's going to fall into the hole.

Notice the form:

Subject + 'be'	+ 'going to'	+ Verb	+ Object
I'm (I am)	going to	play	handball after school.
You're (You are)	going to	be	late for school!

You can also use 'go' with 'going to'!

> I'm going to go home at 3 p.m.
> They're going to go on holiday next summer.

'HAVE TO'

You can use 'have to' to say it is necessary to do something:

> Children have to go to school.
> I have to work from 9 a.m. to 5 p.m.

Notice you use 'has to' with 'he', 'she' and 'it':

> He has to do his homework tonight.

You make the negative with 'doesn't/don't':

> I don't have to work on Saturdays.
> She doesn't have to wear school uniform.

The past is easy. You use 'had to' or 'didn't have to' for everybody:

> In 1992 in Florida, thousands of people had to leave their homes.
> It was a holiday yesterday, so I didn't have to go to school.

Theme E

'COULD': MAKING A REQUEST

You can use 'could' to ask someone to do something:

> Could you answer the phone, please?
> Could you tell me what this word means, please?

You can also use 'could' to ask if you can do something:

> Could I go home early today, please?
> Could I open the window, please?

'WOULD': MAKING AN OFFER

You can use 'would' to offer someone something:

> Would you like a drink of orange?
> Would you like to come to my party?

'ENOUGH'

'Enough' means that there is the right quantity. 'Not enough' means there is less than you want or need.

'Enough' goes *before* a noun:

> There is enough food here for 100 people!
> I haven't got enough money to buy that book.

'Enough' goes *after* an adjective:

> She's not old enough to drive a car.
> The trousers weren't long enough for Tom.

Theme F

PAST CONTINUOUS

You use the Past continuous to describe the background for another action:

> Thousands of people were travelling home when the lights went out.
> I was doing my homework when my friend came to my house.

You can make the negative with 'not' or '–n't':

> He wasn't looking at the cars when he crossed the road.

> Were they singing when the police came?
> Were you watching television when the lights went out?

THE IMPERATIVE

You can use the imperative to give people instructions. To make the imperative we use only the verb (without 'to'):

> Wait here!
> Stay calm!

You can also tell people what they can't do:

> Don't run! Don't shout! Don't make a noise!

You can add 'please' to be more friendly:

> Please hurry! Please come here! Please don't push.
> Please don't shout.

CLASSROOM PHRASES

You can ask for help in your English lessons:

How do you pronounce this word?

Can you repeat that, please?

Can you check this?

How do you say '…' in English?

Sorry, I didn't understand.

Can you look at this? I've finished.

Can you speak more slowly, please?

Can you say that again, please?

Sorry?

INVITING AND SUGGESTING

You can invite someone to do something or go somewhere with you. You can also suggest what you can do:

Why don't you come with me?
Why don't we meet at my house?
Would you like to come?
Shall I tell …?
Let's meet at around five.
See you later.

TALKING ABOUT THE PAST

You can talk and ask about things you did in the past:

Did you have a good weekend?

I had a great weekend, thanks.

What did you do?

I went to the beach.

Who did you go with?

I went with my brother and sister.

What did you do there?

We played football on the beach and swam.

REACTING

You can react to what people say. If you think it is good you can say:

> You lucky thing!
> Brilliant!
> Oh! Fantastic!

If you think it is bad, you can say:

> Oh no!
> Oh, bad luck!
> That's terrible!

EATING OUT – IN A CAFÉ

You can say what you want and ask your friends:

> I'm going to have ...
> I'd like ...
> Can I have ...
> What are you going to have?
> Would you like ...?

ASKING THE WAY

You can ask someone where a place is:

> Excuse me, where can I find a supermarket?
> Excuse me, do you know where the supermarket is?
> Could you tell us where there is a supermarket?

You can answer someone if they ask you:

> I think the nearest supermarket is in Green St.
> It's next to the bus station.
> Sorry, I don't know this town.
> It's in front of the library.

You can give directions:

Turn left.

Turn right.

Go straight on.

Take the second turning on the left.

Take the third turning on the right.

It's on the corner.

Turn left at the traffic lights.

Acknowledgements

The authors and publishers are grateful to the following illustrators and photographic sources:

Illustrators: Sophie Allington: pp.9, 35; Felicity Roma Bowers: pp. 30, 32*t*, 34; Robert Calow: pp. 16*t*, 39, 43, 44*t*, 47, 48, 50, 56; Richard Deverell: pp. 14*t*, 26*t*, 36*t*, 51, 76, 86, 87, 88; Hilary Evans: pp. 18*b*, 31*b*; Gecko Limited: all DTP illustrations and graphics; Peter Kent: pp. 13*b*, 22*b*, 24, 40*b*, 54, 60, 62, 66, 67*t*, 68, 73, 75*t*, 80, 82, 83, 89, 90, 91, 92, 93, 94, 95; Steve Lach: pp. 19, 20, 31*t*, 40*t*, 45, 46, 58*t*, 84, 85; Jan Lewis: pp. 14*m*, 17*b*, 26*m*, 41*b*, 42*b*, 52*b*, 55*b*, 57, 58*b*, 63, 64, 67*b*, 77, 78*t*, 81; Colin Mier: pp. 9, 17*t*, 22*t*, 26*b*, 38*m*, 79*b*; John Plumb: pp. 18*t*, 52*t*; Debbie Ryder: pp. 6*b*, 14*b*, 25*t*, 38*b*, 53*b*, 65*b*, 78*b*; Chris Ryley: pp. 4*tl*, 6*t*, 8, 12, 13*t*, 16*b*, 21, 23, 25*b*, 27, 28, 29, 32*b*, 42*t*, 49, 53*t*, 55*t*, 65*t*, 70, 79*t*; John Storey: pp. 4*tr* & *b*, 5, 10, 11, 36*b*, 37, 38*t*; Mel Wright: pp. 41*t*, 44*b*, 75*b*.

Photographic sources: Action Plus: pp. 14, 15 (Glyn Kirk); Bryan & Cherry Alexander (Paul Drummond): p. 7; John Birdsall Photography: p. 21: Colorific: p. 34*b*; The Hutchinson Library: p. 61*b*; Landmœlingar Islands, Reykjavik: p. 33; Planet Earth Pictures (D. Barrett): p. 34*t*; Scottish Highland Photo Library: pp. 69*t*; Spectrum Colour Library: p. 69*b*; Still Pictures Environmental Picture Library and Agency: pp. 56, 57; Tony Stone Images: p. 61*t*; Derek Pratt/Waterways Photo Library: p. 69*m*.

t = top *m* = middle *b* = bottom *l* = left *r* = right

Picture research by Maureen Cowdroy Picture Research.

Cover design by Dunne & Scully based on an illustration by Felicity Roma Bowers.

Sound recordings by Martin Williamson, Prolingua Productions at Studio AVP.

Freelance editorial work by Edwina Johnson.

Design and production by Gecko Ltd, Bicester Oxon.

Correct sentences for Unit 11, Help yourself with writing: Exercise 2.1

Dinosaurs **lived** millions of years ago.

What's the time**?**

I **am** sitting on a chair.

Yesterday, I **played** football.

Sophie go**es** to school with Barbara.

My brother has got a **big car**.